THE DIVERSITY CONSULTANT COOKBOOK

The Diversity Consultant Cookbook

Preparing for the Challenge

WRITTEN AND EDITED BY

Eddie Moore Jr., Art Munin, *and*
Marguerite Penick-Parks

FOREWORD BY JAMIE WASHINGTON

AFTERWORD BY JOEY IAZZETTO

STERLING, VIRGINIA

Published by Stylus Publishing, LLC.
22883 Quicksilver Drive
Sterling, Virginia 20166-2019

Library of Congress Cataloging-in-Publication Data
Names: Moore, Eddie, Jr., editor. | Munin, Arthur Carl, 1977- editor. |
    Penick-Parks, Marguerite W., 1957- editor.
Title: The diversity consultant cookbook : preparing for the challenge /
    edited by Eddie Moore Jr., Art Munin, and Marguerite Penick-Parks ;
    foreword by Jamie Washington.
Description: First edition. | Sterling, Virgina : Stylus Publishing, 2019. |
    Includes index.
Identifiers: LCCN 2018044590| ISBN 9781620369784 (cloth
    : alk. paper) | ISBN 9781620369791 (pbk. : alk. paper) |
    ISBN 9781620369807 (library networkable e-edition) | ISBN
    9781620369814 (consumer e-edition)
Subjects: LCSH: Educational consultants--United States--Handbooks,
    manuals, etc. | Multicultural education--United States--Handbooks,
    manuals, etc. | School management and organization--United States--
    Handbooks, manuals, etc. | Universities and colleges--United States--
    Administration--Handbooks, manuals, etc.
Classification: LCC LB2799.2 .D58 2019 | DDC 371.2/07--dc23 LC
    record available at https://lccn.loc.gov/2018044590

13-digit ISBN: 978-1-62036-978-4 (cloth)
13-digit ISBN: 978-1-62036-979-1 (paperback)
13-digit ISBN: 978-1-62036-980-7 (library networkable e-edition)
13-digit ISBN: 978-1-62036-981-4 (consumer e-edition)

Printed in the United States of America

All first editions printed on acid-free paper
that meets the American National Standards Institute
Z39-48 Standard.

Bulk Purchases

Quantity discounts are available for use in workshops and
for staff development.
Call 1-800-232-0223

First Edition, 2019

First, I'm forever grateful to my wife and family for their years of ongoing support, patience, and love. Second, this one is for Cooper Street Recreation Center in Punta Gorda, Florida (my hometown). To the haters and motivators, many of my lifelong skills emerged from my time there, and I'm grateful for every experience and lesson learned. Finally, to my good friend and Brotha Thom Determan (deceased). He planted the America & Moore seed in 1995 and has guided, supported, and inspired me over the years to always #MakeItHappen!

Eddie Moore Jr.

This one is for Ava and Vincent. I hope, in some small way, it helps create a more just world for you to live in. And of course, nothing in my life happens without the unwavering support of Heidi. I love you all. Additionally, I would like to thank every person who helped me along the way as a diversity educator and consultant, including Timothy Spraggins, Georgianna Torres Reyes, Vijay Pendakur, Bridget and Rob Kelly, John Dugan, Greg MacVarish, Toby Causby, and Mike O'Sullivan.

Art Munin

As always, the people I have to thank for instilling in me an understanding of my personal responsibility in the field of social justice are my parents, George and Marguerite Penick. It was their love, patience, and years of lessons about inequities in our world that opened my eyes to the need for this work. And as always, I appreciate the unconditional love and support of my daughters, whom I watch follow in my footsteps whether they want to or not, Maggie, Lizbet, Adele, and Danae.

Marguerite Penick-Parks

We all want to give a special thanks to Suzanne Fondrie for her editing expertise in completing this book.

Contents

FOREWORD ix
Jamie Washington

1 SETTING THE TABLE 1
Eddie Moore Jr., Art Munin, and Marguerite Penick-Parks
Lesson 1: The New Consultant Blues 7
Orinthia Swindell
Lesson 2: Community Is Essential 10
Vijay Pendakur
Lesson 3: Managing Emotion 12
Dena Samuels

2 ETHICS INHERENT IN DIVERSITY EDUCATION 17
Eddie Moore Jr., Art Munin, and Marguerite Penick-Parks
Lesson 4: Finding Ways to Continually Check Our Privilege and Hold Ourselves Accountable 21
Diane J. Goodman
Lesson 5: Doing Good Work Can Come With a Target on Your Back 24
Jacqueline Battalora
Lesson 6: Justice, Not Vengeance: Overcoming the Dehumanization of Dysconscious Racism 27
Devon Alexander

3 STARTING YOUR JOURNEY 31
Eddie Moore Jr., Art Munin, and Marguerite Penick-Parks
Lesson 7: Effective Listening: The Secret Sauce of Diversity Consultants 44
John Igwebuike
Lesson 8: There's a Black Man Talking! 47
Bryant K. Smith
Lesson 9: White Man Talking 51
Tim Wise

Foreword

Cooking is one of my favorite pastimes. I grew up in a family of cooks, and preparing a good meal is something that fills me with a great deal of pride, especially when sharing a meal with others. I take time to consider the right ingredients for each dish. I pay attention to the season that we are in and what will satisfy the palate. I'm also attuned to the people who are coming. I don't want to make something that is too rich and spicy for my grandchildren, and I don't want to prepare a dish too "fancy" for my in-laws. These cooking analogies are quite useful as we consider the work of diversity consulting.

When Eddie Moore Jr., Art Munin, and Marguerite Penick-Parks invited me to write this foreword, I was delighted. You see, Moore has had the pleasure of experiencing my home cooking, and he knows that I take seriously not only the preparation but also the presentation and the engaging environment that makes the meal enjoyable and satisfying.

I have had the pleasure and honor of serving as a diversity educator, speaker, and organizational management and culture-change consultant for more than 30 years. During that time, I have watched the need for the understanding of diversity and inclusion issues become more nuanced and complex. When I started my career in 1982, the role of diversity consultant did not really exist in the context of higher education. There were a few people who were doing diversity training sessions, and there was some work happening through human resources to create effective teams, but there was not a group of people who would call themselves "diversity consultants."

Today, as the demand grows for people to have the capacity to work effectively within and across difference, the need for skilled and effective diversity consultants is critical. This book offers important topics to consider if you believe you have what it takes to serve your profession and community in this way. Similar to cooking, just because you have been in a kitchen, watched the cook prepare the meal, and enjoyed it with others, it does not mean you can create that same experience on your own. I have been in many consulting settings and met people who ask, "How do I get to do what you do?" "How did you get into this work?" "How did you prepare for this session?" "What makes a good diversity consultant?" These are all great questions. Many of the answers, along with important perspectives and other topics to consider, are outlined in detail in this cookbook.

Here is the challenge in moving forward: too many people want to read a recipe and race out to open a restaurant the next day. However, they do not do the work necessary to make the dish their own. Comedian Kevin Hart (2013) once said on Twitter, "Everybody wants to be famous, but nobody wants to put in the work." Similarly, many folks want to become diversity consultants, but they often do not lay the foundation required to keep clients coming back or recommending them to others. Becoming a diversity consultant—or a great chef—takes time.

Like the authors, Moore, Munin, and Penick-Parks, when I started this work, I was simply doing what I loved; I was doing what mattered to me. I looked out into the world and saw problems I had the ability to address. I was willing to do whatever it took to address a problem. The problem was injustice. The problem was exclusion. The problem was people were hurting and had no way to talk about it. I did not know that by creating an opportunity on my residence hall floor for men to talk about sexuality and all of its complexities I would be setting the foundation to later be named by the *Economist* as one of the top 10 global diversity consultants. Now that feels like a big deal, and it was. However, that only happened after 25 years of hard work, both inside organizations and as a consultant. When I started I did not know anything about running a business. I did not know anything about the difference between being an in-house diversity change agent and an outside agitator.

I say this so that readers understand that although the demand is greater now than in 1982, the work needed to hone your craft and establish your unique brand is also greater. Don't think you can do this overnight. There is great advice from folks who have traveled the road you are considering—don't take it lightly. Like a recipe in a cookbook, one can move too fast and leave out key ingredients. Sometimes substitutions are okay, but be careful: replacing butter with margarine changes the flavor and outcome. It can be the difference between having a onetime gig or a long-term, multisession, or yearlong contract. The authors have worked in multiple contexts but primarily in education and nonprofit organizations. Although there are transferable skills for other contexts, much of what you will read here is specific to those worlds. This is important as one considers the work necessary to create a sustainable practice.

So let's head into the kitchen and start the process. Remember, don't invite anybody to dinner until you've considered what it takes to prepare this meal. Do you have the necessary space, time, ingredients, and cookware? Is your oven functioning at optimal capacity? Will you need a microwave or simply a stove top? Is this a meal best served cold or at room temperature? *The Diversity Consultant Cookbook* will get you ready, so that you will not only want to serve the meal but enjoy the preparation as well.

Bon Appetit!
Rev. Dr. Jamie Washington
President, The Washington Consulting Group
President and Cofounder, The Social Justice Training Institute
President, American College Personnel Association
Pastor, Unity Fellowship Church of Baltimore

Reference

Hart, K. @KevinHart4Real. (2013, September 21). Everybody wants to be famous, but nobody wants to put in the work [Tweet]. Retrieved from https://twitter.com/kevinhart4real/status/381458979483709440?lang=en

1

Setting the Table

Eddie Moore Jr., Art Munin, and Marguerite Penick-Parks

America is changing. The world is changing. The question is, are we changing? Before you answer, think about this: The majority of the changes are what William H. Frey (2015) refers to as "the browning of America." Racial, cultural, religious, economic, gender, gender identity, and language diversity are becoming more prominent in schools, colleges, universities, communities, churches, workplaces, and other areas of U.S. culture. Recent news stories (Papa John's, Starbucks, H&M, Dove, Kelloggs, etc.) have highlighted examples of people in American society who lack skills and competencies related to diversity, power, privilege, and leadership (Astor, 2017; Bell, 2018; Giammona, 2018; Mcgirt, 2017; West, 2018). In some places, there has been a rise in resistance and incidents of hate (Vara-Orta, 2018). Are we ready? Some people say no, that we don't have a clue. We need help. What should we do? Who has the answers? Where can we get the skills and training needed? Who's the best person or company? We have experienced progress, but there is still a lot of work to do.

When we attend events and conferences throughout the country, we are constantly being asked how we got into the work of diversity consulting. "How do I get started?" people wonder. "What advice can you give someone who wants to have a career as a diversity consultant?" After putting our heads together to expand on and strengthen an idea inspired by Eddie Moore Jr., we realized the answer was clear: there has never been a greater need for more diversity consultants and for this information. Thus, we decided to create this "cookbook."

One of the things we have learned from working in the area of diversity and equity consulting is that, like cooking, it's the little things that will make a significant difference in the final outcome. Perhaps it's a teaspoon or tablespoon of seasoning, or perhaps it's the right temperature or the right amount of time. The smallest inclusion or omission may affect the outcome of the most important meal. In cooking, every step needs to be carefully thought out and carried through.

Diversity consulting is the same. If consultants spend too much time blaming or shaming people instead of developing a welcoming environment and building relationships, the consultant can ruin the presentation before it gets started. Additionally, setting the wrong tone (temperature) may leave the participants deflated, defensive, and angry before the work begins. At that point, nothing may be able to save the presentation (or meal). Or, if your environment has too much sugar, then participants might leave the session not fully understanding the root of the problem; change will never happen, because the problem was never fully explored. You may need more than 60 minutes to discuss race, racism, White privilege, White supremacy, power, privilege, leadership, and oppression in depth. If you only scratch the surface of the core issues, participants might leave the session without enough time and understanding to make an impact or to take action. It is a delicate balance. Like cooking, all ingredients, all steps, all processes must be carefully planned and carried out systematically for success to happen.

That being said, we all know that sometimes the best things come from adding a little more salt, or a pinch of this, or wondering what will happen if you just try something new. That, too, is part of a cookbook. Chefs learn how to explore and grow by trying new things and making adjustments. There is an essence of trial and error in cooking, and there is room for trial and error in diversity consulting. The difference is, when a recipe fails, you throw it out, but when a diversity consulting session goes wrong, irreparable harm can happen—to individuals, to systemic change, to progress, and to your bottom line. That is why having a well-planned and carefully prepared program is key to developing a successful practice.

And, similar to cooking, not everyone has the same palate. There are people who like their food bland and those who like it spicy. Some people cannot stand the texture of yogurt, custard, or tofu, so no amount of sprinkles, granola, or soy sauce will make it something they will eat. Some can smell cilantro from across the room and never try the dish. It may be your taste buds, it may be what you grew up knowing, it may be what you are willing to try, but everyone's food preferences are different. Diversity consulting is like that. Some participants want to dive right into difficult topics, and some want to have a sampling first, just a little at a time. Others may have already been eating a certain spice for years, so it isn't new or different, and they want you to move on. Everyone has a different favorite food or recipe, and everyone is in a different place when it comes to thinking about diversity. It is the job of the consultant to figure out what is needed and how to share it in the best possible way so that as many participants as possible walk away ready to try some more.

One thing we want to be very clear about as you start this book is who the audience is. It is essential that as readers you understand that *The Diversity Consultant Cookbook* is about *how* to become a consultant, not *why* to become one. If you have been drawn to the title, you are already committed to diversity and equity issues. We all come to this work for different reasons and through different paths. In this book you will find the path of its three major authors/ editors.

Also included in this book are personal lessons from well-known and respected consultants who work in the field of diversity, social justice, and equity consulting. Each person has been asked to share a lesson learned from the field to address some of the toughest situations you may face as a diversity consultant. These contributors bring a wide variety of experiences and have encountered issues that may make or break your ability to stay in the field and be successful as a consultant. *The Diversity Consultant Cookbook* is filled with advice from multiple voices, because people in diversity work understand that the more perspectives, the greater the opportunity to create change. Listen to their wisdom and learn from their mistakes, always considering what may or may not work for you, because each contributor has created a personal recipe, as should you.

Like a cookbook, this book is set out in small chunks. Readers will explore how to enhance the skills they have gathered through attending conferences, speaking to groups, and expanding their knowledge base. We address specific marketing issues with ideas on business cards, websites, networking, and even how to dress and how to determine a contract. Because of the inherent controversial nature of discussing issues of diversity, consultants need to be aware of ethical issues that may arise before, during, and after the engagement, and those crucial facets are covered at length. Finally, readers of this work will be able to learn from the positive and negative experiences of not only the three main authors but also of multiple consultants throughout the country.

Building a Strategic Plan

We recommend that as you read through this book, you put together a strategic plan to guide you through your consulting preparation. A strategic plan, similar to preparing a meal, is really just a step-by-step outline with goals. For a strategic plan you need to have a mission, a vision, and goals. You need to consider all three, because they could determine the success of your consulting opportunity. Your mission describes why you exist and what you will do for your customers and is clear and very specific. Don't promise the world . . . promise what you will deliver.

The vision must be just as clear. The vision statement is about where you want to help the organization go. Keep it short, but make it memorable. Once you have decided on the mission and vision, the next step is to do some form of a strengths, weaknesses, opportunities, threats (SWOT) analysis to determine your strengths and weaknesses to prepare for the work that lies ahead. Be honest: no one will see this analysis except you, so the more aware you are of what you know and what you need to know, the better prepared you will be to embark on this journey.

Having laid all of the groundwork, you then set goals, both short term and long term. These goals (the things you hope to accomplish) should be accompanied by objectives (the things you will be able to measure upon completing the training) and then followed by action plans. Where so many people fall down with strategic planning is that they don't set action plans for each objective; they simply set objectives (e.g., participants will learn about racism and power), without stating how they are going to do this. What are the participants going to engage in to "learn" about racism and power, and how will you assess if you have met those goals? It is essential to set action plans for every learning objective. Without the action plans, you have no way to determine if you have accomplished your objectives.

One example would be if you set an objective of engaging in 8 consulting gigs your first year. Make a list of how you're going to find those gigs. Word of mouth? Attend 4 conferences in a year to network? Send out 50 invitations? If you don't set a goal, you don't know what mistakes you may or may not make. To stay with the cooking analogy, if you don't plan ahead to have paprika on hand, your recipe may not work. Consulting is the same: if you don't follow your plan, you may not receive work, and gigs, after all, are the end goal. So make a plan with goals, and if you don't stick to it, you'll at least have a strategic way to see what went wrong and what changes you need to make.

Summary of the Lessons

To support the process of becoming a diversity consultant, we asked professionals in the field to offer advice in multiple areas. As you read, you may notice many contributors saying the same things. This should be taken as emphasizing important ideas rather than being redundant. The first cluster of lessons in chapter 1 reinforces many of the ideas in this introductory chapter. In "The New Consultant Blues," Orinthia Swindell discusses why she chose to begin the process of becoming a consultant after years of "unofficially" working in the field. Because the authors firmly believe that at the core of consulting is building relationships, the second lesson by Vijay Pendakur, "Community Is Essential," supports the importance of community in this work. And the final lesson in the first chapter, "Managing Emotion," by Dena Samuels, reminds the new consultant that first and foremost you must take care of yourself in order to continue in the work.

Chapter 2, on ethics, addresses some of the more difficult aspects of the work: defining *diversity* and your personal decision about how you define your work. To address some of the ethical components of diversity consulting, there are three lessons to support you. The first, "Finding Ways to Continually Check Our Privilege and Hold Ourselves Accountable," by Diane J. Goodman, serves as a reminder of the role of a consultant. In that role, you must always remember that not everyone will appreciate your work and so you must learn to deal with pushback, especially when it becomes public. Jacqueline Battalora also addresses this issue in "Doing Good Work Can Come With a Target on Your Back." Devon Alexander continues the challenge of diversity consulting, especially when race is at the core of the work, in "Justice, Not Vengeance: Overcoming the Dehumanization of Dysconscious Racism."

When starting your journey, chapter 3 explores multiple areas of what it means to be a diversity consultant and information about the body of diversity consultants. Enhancing the material in chapter 3, John Igwebuike opens this cluster of lessons by exploring the importance of being a good listener, a key trait in this field, in "Effective Listening: The Secret Sauce of Diversity Consultants." A pair of lessons by Bryant K. Smith ("There's a Black Man Talking!") and Tim Wise ("White Man Talking") serve as a strong reminder of understanding your role, your position, and when it is essential to exert, or not exert, your privilege. And the final lesson in this cluster, "Be Prepared for Anything and Surprised by Nothing," by Vernon A. Wall, contains multiple gems of advice, from the reminder to hire an accountant to remembering to stay involved in your own personal and professional development.

The final lessons in chapter 4 pull together some additional ideas to think about before getting into the field. "Stress Kills," by Sumun L. Pendakur, addresses an issue faced by everyone at some point, but here it is a pressure heightened by being an active member of the social justice family. What often adds to the stress of being on the road is the family at home, an issue close to the heart of many consultants. Ali Michael addresses this concern in "Radical Politics Made Me Antimotherhood." To remind us all that diversity consulting cannot—and should not—be contained by a nation, Ritu Bhasin engages the reader in the possibilities that global consulting offers in "Global Consulting: Challenges, Opportunities, and Possibilities."

Following the summation in chapter 5, this book includes the words of one of the most important and far-reaching consultants in the field of diversity, equity, power, and privilege—Peggy McIntosh. *The Diversity Consultant Cookbook* concludes with an afterword from Joey Iazzetto that focuses on maximizing the impact of your efforts as a diversity consultant.

References

Astor, M. (2017). *Dove drops an ad accused of racism.* Available from https:// www.nytimes.com/2017/10/08/business/dove-ad-racist.html

Bell, W. K. (2018). *W. Kamau Bell: I know what it's like to get kicked out for being black.* Available from https://www.cnn.com/2018/04/16/opinions/ philadelphia-starbucks-sounds-familiar-to-me-w-kamau-bell-opinion/ index.html

Frey, W. H. (2015, October 19). The browning of America. *Milken Institute Review.* Available from http://www.milkenreview.org/articles/charticle-3

Giammona, C. (2018). *Papa John's chairman Schnatter quits after racial remarks.* Available from https://www.bloomberg.com/news/articles/2018-07-12/ papa-john-s-chairman-schnatter-quits-after-controversial-remarks

Mcgirt, E. (2017). *Kellogg's apologizes for 'racist' corn pops art, says it will be replaced.* Available from http://fortune.com/2017/10/25/racist-corn-pops-box/

Vara-Orta, F. (2018, August 6). Hate in schools. *Education Week.* Available from https://www.edweek.org/ew/projects/hate-in-schools.html

West, S. (2018). *H&M faced backlash over its "monkey" sweatshirt ad: It isn't the company's only controversy.* Available from https://www.washingtonpost .com/news/arts-and-entertainment/wp/2018/01/19/hm-faced-backlash -over-its-monkey-sweatshirt-ad-it-isnt-the-companys-only-controversy /?noredirect=on&utm_term=.34500ecc4064

◆ ◆ ◆ ◆ ◆ ◆

LESSON 1
The New Consultant Blues
Orinthia Swindell

My first thoughts about considering diversity consulting as a full-time gig came to me a few years ago, which means that I really am the new consultant in this group. I was serving as a full-time equity practitioner in a school where I experienced the political culture of the space and the constant undermining of the work by many within the institution. I was well aware of how the effects of this resonated in my body along with the constant weight that I carried around. I knew that something needed to change. Simultaneously, I was also becoming aware that the joy and passion I felt in my initial years as an equity practitioner were waning.

Although I learned early to expect resistance in this work, I felt as if I had hit a wall, due in large part to the marginalization of my work that I experienced, making it impossible for me to do what I'd been charged to do. I began to question myself. Why am I doing this work? Am I really making a difference? Is it worth being on the front lines while being seen as "the problem" within the institution? Should I return to the classroom setting? Each time I questioned myself, I was led back to my belief that this work is an integral part of our growth as human beings and as global citizens . . . that the work I was doing was part of my life's purpose.

→ Questioning helped me clarify my thoughts regarding where I could be most helpful in this work and whether continuing to work within schools was the direction I needed to follow or whether working outside as an independent consultant gave me more leverage. I noticed how consultants I brought to campus were received by the faculty and compared that with how I was received. Some consultants would shed light on and enhance topics that I'd explored with faculty, yet the reception they received differed palpably. This was one of the factors that supported the idea that I needed to explore independent consulting. This led to additional questioning on my part as I began to fit the pieces of the puzzle together. What topics should I facilitate discussions on? Who should I create workshops for? How should I get started? Who should I reach out to for help? The list of questions seemed to grow as I put more thought into this.

→ The journey to clarity about many of the questions has taken a few years. I believe that was due in large part to a combination of feeling a great deal of fear as well as uncertainty. I talked with consultants whose work I admire—a life coach, a spiritual adviser—and each provided me with similar advice.

I realize now that I wasn't always at a place where I could fully receive what was shared with me. My mind was clouded with thoughts related to trying to navigate an institution that touted the rhetoric of being committed to social justice, activism, and diversity but hadn't fully realized what it looked like, along with my personal desire to create spaces for discussions to occur and to help people/institutions/organizations that were in a place of uncertainty, a place that was searching for answers to thoughts and questions centering on race, racism, and the various aspects of identity and how each of these helps to shape and influence people. Through it all, I've learned a great deal, and I'm still figuring things out. A few of the things that I reflect on constantly in my consulting journey follow here. *Transition from story to advice*

Pay Attention to What Excites You

As with any new idea, taking time to contemplate what resonates for you is important. There are tasks required of us that we perform simply because it's part of the course. This may or may not be something that brings you joy. The things that excite you—where you're thinking about various ways to engage the topic and excited about bringing people together around it—are the areas that you should focus on.

Who Is Your Audience?

A consultant once asked me this question, and I responded with silence! This wasn't something that I'd considered, because I was presenting workshops to various audiences. When the opportunity arose for me to seriously consider the question, I responded, "I can work with any audience." The consultant suggested that even though that may be true, it doesn't allow me to focus on being well versed in a particular area. This was difficult for me to hear, and it was something that I needed to sit with. It turned out to be one of the best pieces of advice given to me.

How Should You Narrow Your Focus?

As a creative person, many ideas come to mind frequently, so I have a notepad that I reserve for writing them down. I'm learning to accept the fact that each idea I have will not necessarily come to fruition and that I have to be okay with that. The ideas that are born will lend themselves to conversations and take on a life of their own. Also, should I travel or create a local base for my work? This is not a decision that should be taken lightly, yet is one that can be made keeping in mind what works for you.

Who Can You Identify as a Mentor in This Field?

Attending conferences has provided me with the opportunity to meet many people from different parts of the country. Over the years, my network has expanded, giving me opportunities to connect with a few people who have become mentors for me. I look to them to provide me with insight on my ideas as well as help me to gauge the direction that the work is heading within the larger world. This helps me with creating material that is relevant to various audiences and helps me to have a sense of how I can build on conversations by providing a different vantage point. What's important to keep in mind is that diversity consulting is about so much more than presenting workshops. The road to consulting is a process. I'm still figuring out what works and realizing that what may have worked for someone else may not work for me.

◆ ◆ ◆ ◆ ◆ ◆

LESSON 2
Community Is Essential
Vijay Pendakur

As I prepared to write this reflection, I looked through my files to see when I started getting serious about diversity consulting. It turns out that it's been 10 years! Back then, as a midlevel student affairs professional, I never imagined that organizing trainings, conducting program reviews, and offering keynote speeches would take me all over the United States, from community colleges to elite universities. Nowadays, I have to be selective about the opportunities I say yes to, as I have a wife and 2 small children and a leadership-level role on campus that requires me to stay present for my organization most of the time. But as I think back over this last decade of exciting and challenging work as a diversity consultant, it is quite clear to me that I would not have been as successful as I have been, or as happy with the experience, without a vibrant community of fellow diversity and social justice educators and consultants in my life. Community is essential.

In a functional sense, my community was essential to my success because they were the ones who helped me book my first gigs. Word of mouth from respected colleagues was critical to getting my foot in the door at institutions in the Chicago area, where I was based when I started. These referrals often came from other consultants and trainers who were too busy to say yes to a specific job, so they would recommend me. Alternately, colleagues who weren't consultants but were respected higher education administrators would put my name forward if they heard a committee was searching for a consultant for resident assistant (RA) training or winter leadership renewal. So I would be remiss not to acknowledge the foundational role my community has played in my time as a diversity consultant.

Beyond actually helping me acquire work, my community of higher education practitioners and fellow consultants has served as both a board of advisers and an ideation toolbox over the years. As a board of advisers, they are the people I turn to when I need advice on how to handle a tricky political situation, process a challenging gig when it is complete, or receive feedback on my performance if they have seen me at work. I remember when I booked an RA training in a very rural area in the middle of the country, at an institution with a deep history of conservative politics. The director of residence life told me that the RA group had a lot of returners and that they were still upset about their last diversity training. The consultant the year before had triggered the group in numerous ways. I was also informed that the group was almost all White, 90% male, and heavily conservative Christian. I was anxious about how to structure this daylong training appropriately. I called several people in my board of advisers and asked for advice. They brainstormed with me, talking through how I could modify both my materials and my approach to be successful with the group. This example also demonstrates how members of my community have been critical in assisting me with innovating my curricula and pedagogy, by working as an ideation toolbox at times. When I am looking at a really complicated training or an audience that I am not as comfortable with, I often turn to my community to help me put a fresh set of eyes on the materials I want to use. Or I call colleagues and talk about what I want the audience to learn, and I ask for their ideas on what tools can help engender this learning. In these ways, my community has been essential to my growth as an educator and my long-term success as a consultant.

A final way that my community has been critical to my success as a diversity consultant is as actual partners for the work. When I get called to train a large group, I often ask if I can bring a cofacilitator. This is helpful for crowd management, as it allows us to split the group for more in-depth work. But I've also found it is important for me to partner with other consultants to balance out identities I carry with other identities that might be salient for the audience. So as a heterosexual, able-bodied, middle-class, Asian American man, I want to be thoughtful in bringing a cofacilitator who has different identities, a person who has a complementary approach to training. Without a strong, diverse community of other consultants in my life, I wouldn't have a Rolodex to draw on in these moments, and I know that I wouldn't have been as successful with certain audiences as a result.

From helping me get more work, to serving as a board of advisers or an ideation toolbox, to partnering with me to better engage diverse audiences, my community has been at the heart of my success as a diversity consultant these last 10 years. As I think about doing this work for another decade, it is that community that brings a smile to my face and gives me the necessary resilience to stay committed to the challenging but important work of diversity education for the years to come.

◆ ◆ ◆ ◆ ◆ ◆

LESSON 3
Managing Emotion
Dena Samuels

The work we do as diversity, equity, and inclusion consultants is not only hard work; it is "heart" work. Trainings and workshops on most other subjects focus on the specific content transferred and techniques for implementation. In a diversity and inclusion workshop, asking participants to focus only on content and to leave their hearts at the door is a recipe for disaster.

In order to be effective and inclusive, we must ask everyone to bring their whole selves into the room, and this also means bringing in a fair amount of baggage and highly charged emotions. We all come into the space with myriad social identities, our knowledge and biases about our own and others' social identities, and our experiences—both good and bad—around these identities. Expect challenging emotions to arise, and be prepared for them.

Preempting Challenging Emotions

With the limited time we are typically given with a client or workshop participants, it is especially important to build some trust first before delving into the heart of the subject matter. This will make it more likely that when challenging emotions arise, you will get buy-in from the group regardless of how you choose to deal with the situation. This can take shape through designing deep-diving icebreakers, developing guidelines for effective group engagement, and creating a process for managing volatile situations when they arise.

Addressing Emotional Outbursts

When a biased, offensive comment is made by someone in the group, it is critically important to address it. Many facilitators and consultants have never been trained for this, and because these situations can cause discomfort, the outbursts often go unchallenged, which can create a hostile environment. Mishandling or ignoring the situation, or brushing it off just to get through your original content, can cause significant harm and will be noticed by everyone in the room. This can be a "make or break" moment: facilitators who do not address it often risk losing trust among participants, along with the chance for them to hear anything else you had prepared to present.

Sometimes the comment or behavior is meant to do harm. If this is the case, it is best to spend time unpacking the emotions in the room, inviting participants to share how it feels to hear this type of comment. Reminding participants of your guidelines for effective communication can be useful here.

Many times, the comment is made out of ignorance with no intent to harm; however, that does not lessen the impact of the comment, which is important to address.

Keep in mind that addressing emotional outbursts in the context of antibias workshops or trainings is in fact "doing the work." Consider it an opportunity to model how to engage deeply and build relationships across social differences, and know that it is arguably more important than any other content you hoped to share. Preparing for these challenging situations before they occur is both possible and required for effective diversity, equity, and inclusion work.

There are two processes that must be addressed in responding in this situation: internal and external. The internal process focuses on what is arising in you—whether you are being triggered and, if so, what to do about it. The external process requires reading the room to notice the emotional state of participants and how you will verbally respond to the situation. Start with the internal process before moving on to the external one.

Internal Process

1. Breathe! One mindful deep breath can make the difference between unsuccessfully reacting and effectively responding.
2. Check in with your own emotional and physical well-being. If you are being triggered, you may have some physiological symptoms, such as a quickened heartbeat, a heated face, disorientation, fear, anxiety, and sweaty palms, among others.
3. Breathe again, acknowledging that you are being triggered in this moment.
4. Offer yourself compassion for the difficult situation you are in.
5. Remind yourself that this is an opportunity to practice what you teach.
6. Consider how you might call in the perpetrator of the comment, rather than calling the person out.

External Process

1. Be transparent about your plan. Let the participants know you'd like to unpack the current comment/situation before moving forward with the planned agenda.
2. Remind participants that this is challenging work and that emotions can sometimes arise that we did not expect.
3. Invite participants to consider the offensive comment by responding to your question, "Why might that comment be considered

offensive?" Generalizing in this way takes the attention off the perpetrator, especially if you sense embarrassment from the person. If time permits, participants can answer the question with a partner or by journaling. After the discussion, remember that an apology from the perpetrator is not a requirement for this to be a successful learning moment.

4. Go deeper: Invite participants to consider the social structures that allow offensive comments to be repeated, and often accepted, without question.

5. Rather than giving undue attention to the perpetrator, we can instead focus on the nature of these types of insults and slights, also known as microaggressions, which most often go unchallenged. We can emphasize the importance of interrupting microaggressions whenever we get the chance.

6. Remind participants that part of this work is to acknowledge that we cannot know everything about every social identity and, therefore, based on the pervasive and often reckless misinformation we are provided daily by society, we will make mistakes. To be effective in diversity and inclusion work, we must show up to do the work again anyway. Again, and again.

Finally, no matter how you feel you handled the situation, remember that this is difficult work and that the more practice you have dealing with challenging situations, the better prepared you will be. This is not the time to berate yourself for mishandling the situation but rather to congratulate yourself for taking action and doing the best you could in the moment. Do your homework in advance by considering scenarios and how you will manage them. It's not an *if*, it's a *when*. Challenging emotions are guaranteed in diversity work. This work is not for the faint of heart but rather for the heartfelt. With some forethought, you can be well prepared to manage whatever emotions arise.

2

Ethics Inherent in Diversity Education

Eddie Moore Jr., Art Munin, and Marguerite Penick-Parks

Consulting is one thing, but diversity consulting comes with its own issues. It can be complex, because you are dealing with a subject that many people in your audience and in the field consider difficult. You're asking people to engage in a subject many don't want to talk about and others don't think they need to talk about. The editors of this volume have all received hate mail at some point and have often been challenged by session participants. If you have made it this far into the book, you are committed to the field and already recognize the challenges. The following recommendations can help guide your steps into the unique field of diversity consulting.

What Does Diversity Mean?

It is essential to define *diversity, social justice, equity,* and other terms that may identify exactly who you are as a consultant. What is your particular area of expertise? What is your specific focus? As consultants we all come to this work with a variety of focuses. Therefore, when you say you are a diversity consultant, what do you mean? If *diversity* means "difference," then what does it mean to you? To one person the consulting may be centered on "diversity" in the sense of race; to another it may mean "inclusion." To some people it is a means to equity, whereas others consider their end goal to be social justice. Are you going to focus on issues of intersectionality, or are you asking your audience to engage specifically in race issues?

And can you talk about race without bringing in class? It is acceptable to combine those terms in your identity development, but you have to know what your focus is; what your definitions are; and, hence, what you are going to deliver.

Let's take a look at definitions associated with words commonly used by people considering becoming diversity consultants. We ask you to think about how you define each of the following and what you consider your specific area(s) of expertise. Our goal is to be certain you establish your personal consulting identity, because we find that the following terms are very different across the field.

Diversity

The term *diversity* in and of itself simply means difference or dissimilar. It is the act of putting this term into a socialized context where things differ—or where there are "differences," especially in relation to issues of power and privilege—that the word takes on a dynamic and inextricable meaning.

Social Justice

Paul Gorski, a prominent consultant in the field, makes a sound argument for recognizing the need not to co-opt words and use them interchangeably or as catch phrases. In his article "Social Justice: Not Just Another Term for 'Diversity'" (Gorski, 2013), he explores the evolution of terms as they became part of the mainstream mantra. He challenges us to recognize what is at the heart of social justice: "Social justice is the inverse of social injustice. So the results of my social justice work should be less injustice." Think about that as a constant in your recipe book.

Equity

Gorski defines *inequity* as

> an unfair distribution of material and nonmaterial access and opportunity. Material access refers to access to things that cost money: technology, tutors, etc. Nonmaterial access refers to social and culture conditions, like access to a curriculum that reflects people like me, access to school policy that protects my interests, etc. Equity,

then, is a process of redistributing access and opportunity fairly. In that sense, equity is the absence of bias and inequity, the absence of racism, sexism, and so on., in policy, practice, and every aspect of schooling. (P. Gorski, personal communication, August 25, 2018)

Inclusion

Inclusion may be viewed differently depending on the field. In K–12 education, it refers to the inclusion of students with special abilities in the "regular" education classrooms. The current terminology prevalent in higher education is *inclusive excellence*, which entails inclusion of everyone, including, but not specific to, those with special abilities.

Cultural Competency

There are many ways to define *cultural competency*; however, we choose to reference global consultant Ritu Bhasin, who later in this book defines *cultural competence* as one's ability to notice behavioral differences tied back to culture and cultural identity. It's about noticing those differences, understanding those differences, being judgement neutral about those differences, able to break those differences, leverage those differences, and adapt to those differences.

Privilege

Privilege refers to the unearned advantages and entitlements one group possesses over another based simply on identity. It is a competitive edge that is often invisible to those who hold it but that is apparent to members of the outgroup (Johnson, 2005).

This book is not about telling you how to define these terms or others. This is your recipe. But you need to know what to put in your recipe, so you need to know how *you* define the terms. Be clear; be specific; and, whenever possible, ground your terminology in literature, research, and theory. In diversity consulting, it is easy for participants who want to disagree with a presentation to argue with emotions, but it is not as easy for them to argue with research-based ideologies. Think about what these terms mean through the lens of consulting and/or what they mean to you through the lens of being a consultant. When communicating with potential clients, be certain you are using the same terminology as the people who wish to offer you a contract. You do not want to show up with a steak if they are all vegetarian. You have to be on the same page: does *diversity* mean the same to both of you?

As a consultant it is essential that you are always aware of your privilege and always check it. Who gets booked? Who doesn't get booked? Everyone in the field has some type of privilege, because you have made it this far. But not everyone has the same amount of privilege, and, generally, those who have the most are White. But White is not always right and not always the voice that needs to be heard. We often see White social justice educators receiving more opportunities to provide consulting on diversity topics. That may mean that White people are the ones profiting at the expense of groups already marginalized. So as a consultant, as a *diversity* consultant, what can you do to change the environment? How can you include many perspectives, amplify silenced voices, and help those voices benefit from your connections? Think about how you can develop a conscious strategy around your mission and vision when it comes to partnering or securing consulting gigs. Cooking together is more interesting than cooking alone, and more ideas come from two sets of taste buds and experiences. How can you use your privilege to empower and privilege others? Isn't that really the ethical reason for doing this work? Isn't giving a voice, giving power, giving privilege the best way to turn social injustice into social justice? What a great way to give back!

Finally, take care of yourself: exercise, meditate, reflect. If you are the tool, you must stay healthy, and being a diversity consultant is not without its stressors. Listen to positive inspirational music or spoken word, something that refuels you with positive energy and thoughts. Continue educating yourself by attending sessions at conferences, not only for connections but also for your personal growth. And lean on each other. The people who have given their time to this book are there for you. Others are there for you. We need to stick together, not work against each other. Believe us, there is enough work out there.

References

Gorski, P. C. (2013, February 19). Social justice: Not just another term for "diversity." *The CSJE Blog* (Commission for Social Justice Education).

Available from https://acpacsje.wordpress.com/2013/02/19/social-justice-not-just-another-term-for-diversity-by-paul-c-gorski/

Johnson, A. G. (2005). *Privilege, power, and difference* (2nd ed.). Boston, MA: McGraw-Hill.

LESSON 4
Finding Ways to Continually Check Our Privilege and Hold Ourselves Accountable
Diane J. Goodman

When people tell us to "check our privilege," they are asking us to be aware of how being part of a privileged group has shaped us and given us advantages denied those from a marginalized group. Accountability asks us to consider the impact of our work (not just our intentions); its alignment with social justice goals; and our responsibility to others, most importantly those from marginalized groups. Additionally, we need to take into account concerns raised about consultants benefiting from their privilege. Most of us are part of both privileged and oppressed groups and may be consultants on a range of issues. Given the intersectionality of our various identities, our privileged identities affect us whether or not we are addressing an issue as part of a dominant group or working on issues related to our marginalized identities. For example, as a White woman, my Whiteness and White privilege come into play when I'm doing an antiracism workshop as well as a workshop on sexism. In all cases, we need to be mindful of the significance of our privileged identities and the responsibility that carries.

What follows are reflection points for all diversity consultants.

Do Our Own Work—Continually

Before anyone from a privileged group is in the role of educator or consultant, we need to have done deep exploration of how that privilege manifests in society and in our own lives. This includes examining our own societal conditioning and ways we enact our internalized superiority. We need self-awareness and the ability to self-reflect on our behavior.

Solicit Feedback and Engage With Humility

In addition to our own self-awareness and self-monitoring, we need the perspectives of others. There are numerous ways we can get feedback on how we show up and do our work to help us check our privilege.

Utilize Evaluations From Participants

What are people saying about our content, skills, and facilitation style? We can ask specific questions to elicit helpful feedback, such as "How well does the facilitator embody the qualities of equity and inclusion being addressed?" or "How aware and knowledgeable is the facilitator on these issues?" In particular, consider what people from marginalized groups say.

Debrief With the Organizers of the Training

After the workshop or consulting work, talk with organizers (who are often from marginalized groups or from privileged groups with high awareness) about how they experienced working with us, particularly as someone with a dominant group identity. How did they feel about the planning process and our facilitation?

Check In With Cofacilitators

If we are cofacilitating, especially in a mixed-identity team, have conversations about how we work together and deal with our privilege. Check in throughout and at the end about the process. In order for people to be honest with us, we need to engage with humility and a willingness to learn. If we truly care about being effective change agents, this feedback is invaluable.

Acknowledge and Support People From Marginalized Groups

Sometimes we are given opportunities because we are members of privileged groups. Often I am brought in as a consultant by people from marginalized groups because they feel others from a privileged group can better hear from or relate to someone who shares their dominant identity. Yet we need to be careful not to reinforce inequitable power dynamics and instead amplify the voices of people from marginalized groups.

Acknowledge People We've Learned From

None of us just figured this stuff out by ourselves. People from dominant groups learn about systemic inequities from people from oppressed groups. Reference these individuals and the work that has informed your own analysis and understanding.

Don't Take Credit for Ideas That Aren't Our Own

This is especially true when ideas originated with people from marginalized groups. Intentionally include and highlight the contributions of oppressed groups and give credit where credit is due.

Reference and Reinforce the Work Marginalized Groups Are Doing in the Organization With Whom We Are Consulting

As opposed to coming in as the outside expert, approach our relationship with clients from marginalized groups as a partnership. Discuss how to acknowledge, build on, and support the work they are doing within their organization.

Open Doors, Share Privilege

Consider how to use the privilege we have to open doors and create more equity and inclusion.

Increase Access to Opportunities and Visibility for People From Marginalized Groups

Cofacilitate in organizations or copresent webinars and at conferences to give people from marginalized groups visibility and enable them to become known. Make consulting referrals and promote the work of individuals from marginalized groups with organizational leaders or conference organizers with whom you have a relationship.

Contribute to Social Justice Efforts of Marginalized Groups

There are a variety of ways to share the benefits of being consultants with privileged identities. For example, we can contribute a percentage of the money earned from our consulting to social change groups led by people from oppressed groups. We also can offer our particular areas of expertise or access to social power to support their work.

Most importantly, we need to be self-reflective and in conversation with people who share our commitment to social justice, with similar and different social identities, to help us figure out how to continually check our privilege and remain accountable. How we do the work is part of the work.

◆ ◆ ◆ ◆ ◆ ◆

LESSON 5
Doing Good Work Can Come With a Target on Your Back
Jacqueline Battalora

Ingredients of Good Work

Professional support (at least one)
Friends (two or three will do)
Conviction (a strong variety)
Personal investment
Common sense

You are unlikely to challenge structures of oppression without facing resistance. Those who reap the benefits of the status quo will defend their perceived rights and interests. As someone who has been addressing structural inequality since the 1990s through a lens that highlights the workings of White superiority, I have known this resistance well. It has manifested in classic White fragility, in offensive and abusive communications, and sometimes in threats of violence. Not much work that is worthwhile comes without a cost.

Following my keynote address to an audience of more than 2,000 people, the hate mail arrived en masse. I heard pieces of my address on national television in an "undercover" Fox News segment covered by Megyn Kelly, where my work was taken out of context and represented as state-sanctioned propaganda. Messages included threats to the conference, its organizers, the host city, and the teachers union. One e-mail message read, "You and your conference are sick and demented progressive garbage. Go F_ _ _ yourselves, we should burn down Madison and blow up AFT [American Federation of Teachers] headquarters" (C. Leland, personal communication, May 12, 2014, derogatory language adjusted). Another message stated, "I know WE are doing everything we can to spread your stupidity around the country and make everyone aware exactly who you are. Keep going!" (R. Jackson, personal communication, February 7, 2014).

Although I would love to claim that I have not been impacted by these experiences, nothing would be further from the truth. The impact, however, is not only negative. Each hate message and threat made my stomach churn, made my heart race, and evoked monsters in my imagination. Indeed, I am human, and it is much more enjoyable to be liked. But lucky for me, I live with a labor organizer who repeatedly stands up to Goliath, who in the face of ferocious demonization stands tall, guided by principles of respect, dignity, and justice. I have witnessed the personal attacks and demonization intensify exactly when labor organizing work is most effective, galvanizing the base and exposing injustices to the larger community. In other words, I know that when your work is attacked, especially by those groups and individuals aligned with White supremacy ideology, you have struck a chord. No one wastes energy on you or your work when it is irrelevant. When you pose a threat to White supremacy, they lash out.

Receiving hate mail and even threats from groups and organizations aligned with White supremacy ideology is a significant acknowledgment of success. Although the initial impact can feel like a punch in the stomach, it means a huge congratulations is in order not only for work well done but also effective work, impactful work—work that is challenging the core structures of inequality.

Instructions

Upon receipt of hate mail, communicate immediately with a colleague who supports your work. Share the communication and spend time talking about the message. In a large bowl, mix up this professional support with support from friends. Again, share the message and talk through your feelings, concerns, and fears. Be sure to add conviction and your personal investment to the mix. Articulate why you care so deeply about the work. Affirm those convictions and express the reasons that the work is valuable to you. For example, I know that dismantling White supremacy means freedom for me, a White person. It means freedom from delusions of grandeur, from unfair receipt of resources within a national narrative of equality, and it means the ability to empathize with and love humans who are often referred to as people of color. I am in this work of dismantling White superiority to save myself, to forge a better future for my family and the planet we share.

Sprinkle common sense as needed. If there is any threat, contact local law enforcement and file a complaint. I recommend sharing a copy of any hate message or threat with your superior at work and with the organization's public safety department. If you are self-employed, have a colleague in the field serve as the holder of these communications on your behalf. But remember, it is important that you contact local and perhaps federal law enforcement in the event of any actual threat. Don't take unnecessary risks. If you present at night, ask a group to walk with you to your car. Trust your gut. Call for help when you need it. After receiving a threatening message, communicate with neighbors and ask that they help keep an eye out. Pop in to the local police station and talk about the threat and your concerns. My local police department responded by having a squad car pass my home regularly. If fear is taking over, a dog that is trained for protection can be an amazing comfort and a companion.

I cannot promise you that no physical harm will ever come to you for doing social justice work. The best protection, though, is a strong community of colleagues, friends, and neighbors, along with tenacious convictions and clarity about your personal investment in the work. Common sense will help you take wise action including when to involve law enforcement.

◆ ◆ ◆ ◆ ◆ ◆

LESSON 6
Justice, Not Vengeance: Overcoming the Dehumanization of Dysconscious Racism
Devon Alexander

Time and time again individuals engaged in racial equity work share with me their experiences of people with whom they work accosting them with vehement defensive and combative statements about race:

> "I work here because it is racially diverse!"
> "Talking about race is the problem. If we didn't talk about it, then it wouldn't be a problem!"
> "You're the one making waves and causing problems with all your talk about race."
> "How dare you accuse me of enacting racism; I'm not racist! You're the racist!"

I have spent 10 years learning not to respond to individuals who lash out through these statements in ways that distort my integrity and character as a racial equity leader. This, however, has been a learning process in which I have been teetering on the edge of allowing dark vengeance to consume me. Though the process has been excruciating, the righteous growth of my character as a racial equity leader and individual outweighs the pain along the journey. This piece is written for individuals who feel the pull away from engaging in the work of racial equity with courage, grace, and compassion. Your character and integrity as a racial equity leader and individual can be safeguarded against the pervasive corruption of dehumanizing White supremacy.

An uncritical habit of mind, an impaired consciousness, and a distorted way of thinking about the social construction of race ("White superiority" and "color inferiority") and racism have an impact on racial equity leaders. White supremacy, which is inherent in the defensive and combative attacks of individuals enacting dysconscious racism, reflects an uncritical habit of mind (perceptions, attitudes, assumptions, beliefs) that justifies inequity and exploitation by accepting the existing order of things as a given.

Dysconscious racism is an attempt to maintain the racialized identity of those who attack us. It is an understandable response to desire to retaliate when you experience attacks on your dysconscious racism. However, racial equity leaders must ensure that they do not allow their character to become distorted and misaligned due to the racialized projections of racially dysconscious individuals. Do not repay the dehumanizing self-centeredness of their dysconscious racism with your own self-centered retaliatory combativeness. Retaliating corrupts the work of justice upon which racial equity work is founded. The work of racial equity is designed to shift the normed U.S. unhealthy racial discourse and engagement patterns. Discarding the pursuit of healthy racial engagement in exchange for retaliatory combative racial engagement results in the failure of racial equity work.

The defensive and combative attacks of U.S. sociosystemic dehumanizing White supremacy will be manifested against you. When working with individuals within institutions who proclaim commitment to identifying, investigating, and eliminating systemic racial disparities, inequities, and injustices, the habitual experience of being attacked for engaging in and leading racial equity work can be overwhelming, debilitating, and disheartening. Too often, racial equity leaders express experiencing burnout and despair. Although the incongruity of word and action regarding racial equity is a pervasive reality, racial equity leaders can strategically prepare to experience, face, counter, and overcome this lack of racial integrity of individuals and institutions. Racial equity leaders can investigate their racial discourse and engagement patterns in order to find places of stability to challenge racial inauthenticity, dysconsciousness, and deceit. Through this process, racial equity leaders can overcome their patterns that are not fortified against the manifestation of dysfunctional U.S. racial culture within themselves. Racial equity leaders can find within themselves the expressions and engagement patterns that reflect the internalized racial dysfunction of individuals with whom we navigate in the work of racial equity and justice. This critical racial self-reflection opens the pathway to holding yourself, individuals, and institutions accountable for racial equity work with grace and compassion. Racial equity leaders can also locate healthy boundaries that provide opportunities for progressive strategic cultivation of more authentic and courageous racial equity collaboration, community, and leadership within their work.

Justice is not vengeance. Justice seeks truth, what is right and fair, and healthy engagement. Vengeance is what results after all efforts for justice have been denied and thwarted. Racial equity workers must ensure that they have manifested their integrity and character in the work of racial equity in an uncorrupted spirit of justice. We can overcome the dehumanizing evil of dysconscious racism and White supremacy with the good, righteous, and humanizing work of racial equity. Though it is challenging, given the vehement defensiveness and combative attacks that are leveled against us, fortifying and manifesting your racial equity integrity and character firmly rooted in justice will result in progressive victories that will transform you, others, and your institutions in ways that will bring about racial equity and racial justice.

As it says in Romans 12:17–19, 21,

[17] Do not repay anyone evil for evil. Be careful to do what is right in the eyes of everyone. [18] If it is possible, as far as it depends on you, live at peace with everyone. [19] Do not take revenge, my dear friends[.] . . . [21] Do not be overcome by evil, but overcome evil with good. (Biblica, New International Version)

3

Starting Your Journey

Eddie Moore Jr., Art Munin, and Marguerite Penick-Parks

Defining what exactly a *diversity consultant* is may be one of the most difficult aspects to this text. After all, there is not a singular road that leads professionals to this line of work. Additionally, there is not just one type of work that can fall under the umbrella of consulting. Everything from a onetime workshop to an extensive program review exists in the world. But, nonetheless, because it exists, we have to find a way to define it.

A *consultant*, in the most general terms, "is a person in a position to have some influence over an individual, [a] group, or an organization, but who has no direct power to make changes or implement programs" (Block, 2000, p. 2). So, in other words, a consultant is a professional from outside an organization who has knowledge, skills, and abilities but no positional authority to create change inside of an organization.

What consultants bring to the table are abilities that typically fall into three categories. First, consultants have technical skills to add something of value or answer a question that an organization has. This may mean the consultants have credentials or experience that is lacking in the unit. Second, consultants carry strong interpersonal skills. They have the ability to make abstract or complicated ideas tangible and real to participants. Third, and perhaps the most obvious, are the consulting skills a professional must have to be successful (Block, 2000). If the organization wanted to, it could hire a permanent employee to give the organization what the consultant brings. There is a special reason why it has chosen to bring someone from the outside to help. This can be a vulnerable choice for an organization, and successful consultants muster all of their expertise and communication skills to create a valuable experience. Furthermore, consultants must also work to ensure that the organization can continue in a positive direction after they depart.

A *diversity educator*, in contrast, is a knowledgeable and skilled change agent or catalyst for change who works for an organization such as an institution of higher education or not-for-profit. Within the context of higher education, there are positions where these responsibilities are explicitly detailed in the job description and often exist in multicultural affairs offices or other departments such as residence life. Additionally, there are some officials who fulfill the duties of diversity educators even though it is not formally stated. From the perspective of one of the editors (Munin), this is the role he has found himself in throughout his career, and he considered it beneficial to have a leader from the dean of students office active in this work. It exemplifies that one does not need a prescribed role to be part of making a campus a more inclusive place.

A *diversity consultant* brings all of the talents and nuance of being a consultant and melds it with the specialized skills of being a diversity educator. The end product is a professional working in a unique enterprise that seeks to effect positive social change in organizations.

Despite knowing what a diversity consultant is, how you become a diversity consultant requires further exploration. In considering the topic, this chapter examines who these professionals are through a survey of current diversity consultants. The chapter then covers specific topics on the journey toward becoming a diversity consultant and ends with advice and encouragement to those starting out.

Who Are Diversity Consultants?

Because no organization exists that gathers information on who exactly diversity consultants are, the editors of this book sought to collect data on those in the field. A survey was constructed and shared via e-mail and social media in order to capture the broadest sample of those operating as diversity consultants. Of course, surveys, including this one, are inherently imperfect. But we would do well to remember the words of mathematician George E. P. Box, who said, "All models are wrong, but some models are useful" (Box & Draper, 1987, p. 424). This quote encapsulates that all theories, all surveys, and all data sets are imperfect and, therefore, wrong. However, that does not mean that they are not useful.

This survey generated 18 responses, and what follows are the data offered by those participants. It should be noted that for every demographic category, respondents were offered many options to select from as well as the ability to enter their own response. The information reported here reflects the data gathered, not the totality of potential responses. Table 3.1 outlines the years of experience as a diversity consultant the respondents reported (2 participants did not answer this question). Figure 3.1 shows the highest degree earned for diversity consultants. Table 3.2 details their fields of study for their highest degree earned. Figure 3.2 exemplifies whether their work as a diversity consultant is full- or part-time. Figure 3.3 reports age, Figure 3.4 reports

TABLE 3.1
Experience as a Diversity Consultant

Years of Experience	Responses
1–5	5
6–10	3
11–15	5
16–20	1
21–25	2

Figure 3.1. Highest degree earned by respondents.

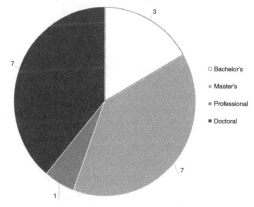

□ Bachelor's
▣ Master's
▪ Professional
▪ Doctoral

TABLE 3.2
Field of Study for Highest Degree Earned

Field	Responses
Biology	1
Business Administration	1
Counseling	1
Education	3
Higher Education Administration	5
Journalism	1
Law	1
Multicultural Education/Social Justice	1
Natural Sciences	1
Organizational Leadership: Adult Learning and Leadership	1
Philosophy and Social Policy	1
Sociology	1

Figure 3.2. Full-time or part-time status as a diversity consultant.

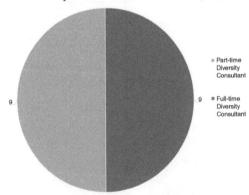

race, Figure 3.5 reports sexual orientation of survey respondents, and Table 3.3 reports gender of survey respondents.

As these data sets suggest, there is incredible diversity in who diversity consultants are. Additionally, there is not a singular path for how a person becomes a diversity consultant. For some it occurs through educational programs directly tied to the field, whereas others have

Figure 3.3. Age of respondents.

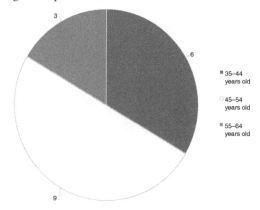

Figure 3.4. Race of respondents.

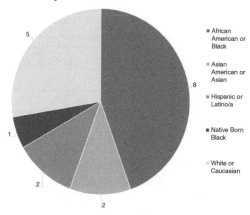

degrees in natural sciences and biology. For those who want to become diversity consultants, this may be disheartening. After all, it would be a lot easier if this chapter could articulate a single path for embarking on this endeavor. Although such clarity may appear easier, the wide possibilities underscore a vital and meaningful reality: diversity consultants are made, not born. A single path would mean that only certain people can do this work, which is not the case. The divergent paths that we have walked exemplify how people doing this work reflect the diversity of the world we are attempting to change. And that is a very good thing.

Figure 3.5. Sexual orientation of respondents.

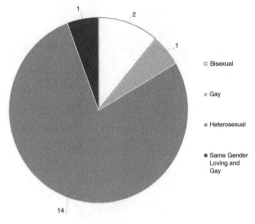

TABLE 3.3
Gender of Respondents

Gender	Number of Respondents
Female	9
Male	9

Getting Started

Although one path does not exist, there are a series of discussion points and aspects of advice that will assist prospective diversity consultants as they begin their journey.

Knowledge Versus Skills

What do diversity consultants need to be successful? Do they need in-depth topical knowledge as it relates to diversity and social justice or the skills to facilitate complex and controversial topics? Of course, the only real answer is that a successful diversity consultant needs both. However, that is far easier said than done. Anyone who has been in higher education has endured a course where a professor was highly knowledgeable about the topic at hand yet lacked the ability to teach effectively. In contrast, there are examples of diversity workshops where it was obvious that the presenter had fantastic presentation skills, but when subjected to difficult questions at the core of the issue, the consultant faltered in the ability to respond. Either scenario can be damaging to our movement toward positive social change. One participant in our survey shared, "When people have negative learning experiences, they often stigmatize the content and not the unskilled facilitator." Such an outcome can affect people and organizations for years to come.

As the data earlier in this chapter show, there is no single field or educational trajectory that leads a person to become a diversity consultant. However, many in this field have educational backgrounds in education and the social sciences. Often in that educational journey there is specific attention paid to the critical lens. In education that could be critical race theory. In communications or sociology it could be social dominance theory. In gender studies it could be feminist theory. Whatever the field, there is an underpinning of critical ideology that must be learned, understood, and applied to diversity consulting efforts. After all, as Audre Lorde (2007) so eloquently stated, "The master's tools will never dismantle the master's house" (p. 110). It is essential for a diversity consultant to learn how the hierarchy is supported and perpetuated to avoid becoming an unwitting accomplice. In reflecting on the work of a diversity consultant, one survey participant challenged us to reflect on how "White supremacy is baked in" to this work.

With diversity consultants being overrepresented with academic backgrounds in education and the social sciences, there is the potential for a blind spot in our field. Any field of study has norms—ways of learning and investigating or, put more simply, a culture. The culture draws in people who tend to be like-minded and seek to understand the world in similar ways. For instance, many who are students of the social sciences, particularly psychology and counseling, are moved and drawn in by the power of stories. This leads many to a deep respect and appreciation for critical race theory and counternarrative storytelling. After all, stories are powerful, and the stories of groups who are often silenced must be brought forth and understood in order for true change to occur. However, all people do not learn or seek to experience the world in this manner. If this is the only educational tool in our toolbox, we could be failing to reach participants who have more fact-based learning preferences. As diversity consultants, we all need to understand the assets of our educational backgrounds while also attending to the deficits or gaps that are present in every field of study.

As a final point on education, we offer some thoughts relating to the diplomas many people have hanging on their walls. As seen from the data reported, achievement in higher education appears to correlate with those in this field. This is true not only because of the knowledge gained through degree programs but also because those pieces of paper open doors. Diplomas are unique entities in that way. Very rarely are you able to attain something that remains valuable throughout your life. The authors of this book are continuing to benefit from the value of degrees they earned 10, 15, even 20 years ago. The power of that piece of paper does not diminish over time. However, people who have stopped seeking learning opportunities after graduation eventually are exposed. It is incumbent on all of us to continue learning, to continue seeking new experiences, and to continue developing who we are trying to be. This is not a field for resting on your laurels, and being content can mean becoming complacent. We need to find new ways to challenge ourselves or else those degrees just become pieces of paper.

As we state from the outset, all of the knowledge and academic credentials in the world will not be useful to a diversity consultant if that person cannot translate complex ideas to an audience and facilitate contentious conversations. To build this vital skill set throughout the educational journey, we recommend seeking out opportunities where you can participate in these conversations. Focus on finding your voice and on how to convey ideas so others understand. Furthermore, as you refine that skill set, also spend time training your mind to not only listen to what people are saying but also hear what they are communicating. Those are often two different things. For instance, one lesson learned from the field of counseling regards the exploration of anger. For obvious reasons, dealing with an angry person can be unsettling or triggering. Often when we communicate with a person in an angry state, we respond only to the anger and bang against it like a wall. However, anger is an emotion that cannot exist on its own. It can exist only because something else is feeding it, such as hurt or fear. Speaking to that hurt or fear can help defuse a situation and increase the odds of a positive outcome. An effective diversity consultant will develop the skills to speak to the root of an issue that a person is communicating, not simply the words said.

Additionally, a diversity educator must be an effective public speaker, a person who can lead a group on a journey. We need to reach everyone . . . the person who is excited to get started and the person who is present because his or her boss required it. Much like a new pilot needs to accrue flight hours, a diversity consultant needs to get in front of people early and often. In the beginning, speak anywhere you can get an opportunity. If you attend a conference, submit three proposals to get practice and exposure. Contact student organizations and nonprofits and volunteer to lead a workshop. Seek out practicing diversity consultants and ask to shadow them for a day. Attend workshops, to learn what to do (and what not to do) when engaging an audience. Put time, thought, and energy into contemplating how an audience is going to respond to your workshop or presentation. As Shakespeare (2018) said in *As You Like It*, "All the world's a stage" (p. 56) and successful diversity consultants intentionally and thoughtfully prepare their scenes.

A final note on this section: as you engage with the field, you begin to build your own workshop and presentation materials. Of course, all of us start from what has already been developed and take it in new directions, so make sure you are giving credit to and seeking permission from individuals when you adapt their work. One of the authors attended a workshop many years ago with a colleague. Halfway through, that colleague turned to the author to comment that he was impressed by the materials presented. The author replied that he agreed wholeheartedly. In fact, he thought they were good when *he* wrote them. There was not a single word of credit given.

Learn From Your Failures

Early in Munin's career, he accepted a contract with a higher education institution that wished to have a cross section of its leaders participate in a daylong retreat. The retreat would cover topical, tangible information as well as experiential activities aimed at heightening their understanding of diversity, in addition to building their sense of team. This was his first contract where some of the participants would be high-ranking institutional executives, and he was nervous, to say the least.

For almost the entire day, the retreat went phenomenally well. Munin engaged participants and met the goals he set. As the day drew to a close, he was feeling pretty good about himself and the job he had done. The group was a little ahead of schedule; the day was looking like it was going to end about 10 minutes early. Instead of just closing out the work, he drew the 20 or so participants in a circle for a final reflection on the day. He asked participants to go around in a circle and share 1 thought about how they felt about the day. Munin stated further that no one would comment on or question what was shared, as he wanted them to express their thoughts freely. He sat back confident in his belief that he was about to hear every person offer glowingly positive reflections. A person jumped in to start, and around the circle they went. Person after person talked about how ecstatic he or she was about what was accomplished and his or her excitement for the forward momentum his or her diversity efforts would have after the retreat. The group made it all the way around the circle, to the final person. What she shared will be seared into Munin's mind forever; she stated, "Something happened early on today that I do not want to go into detail about. But it cast a shadow over this whole retreat, and I do not know if I can work here anymore after this."

That comment sucked all the air out of the room. Munin was stunned, to put it mildly. In addition to processing the comment, he was pondering a conundrum: he set up the impromptu sharing session with the guideline that no one could respond to what was shared. It was meant to be a purely open space.

There are many things to be learned from this failure. One of the most central lessons is that when you are working with a group you must be constantly asking yourself a series of questions:

- Who is not engaged?
- Who is marginalized?
- Who is not being heard?
- Who do I not see?
- Where are my blind spots?

In any group you work with, there will be people who exist inside of these questions. It is our duty to speak to them as well, not just those who are heaping praise on us.

Fixating on our successes will take us only so far. We need to examine critically where we fall short of our goals and how we contribute to that situation. None of us are perfect, and failures are inevitable. Munin spent a long time beating himself up for the incident, but in the end, all he could do was own his mistake with that client, attempt to make amends, and use the situation as a learning experience.

Fake It 'Til You Make It

Two truths guide this subsection. First, we are all imposters. Every diversity consultant has, at some point, wondered why organizations should allocate a portion of their budget to hire him or her. Second, there is nothing unique about those who do this work, although some people may disagree. This false belief could lead to other potential diversity consultants self-selecting out of this work, believing that they are not, somehow, qualified. Simply put, there is nothing inherently special about the people who do this work. That idea is a cognitive and emotional hurdle you may need to deal with before starting this journey.

As to the first point, imposter syndrome is real. People who battle this phenomenon "find themselves trapped in a cyclical behavior pattern that reinforces the belief that their successes are not due to their own abilities" (Cowman & Ferrari, 2002, p. 120). These individuals worry that others will find out that they are frauds or not worthy of the position they have attained. Unfortunately, this is often not an issue a professional battles only once. However, although imposter syndrome may surface from time to time, it can get easier to thwart its effects. The cure is not necessarily convincing yourself that you are not an imposter. Although we'd hope to know in our hearts that this is not actually the case, more often than not it can be easier to start with a parallel truth: we are *all* imposters. Each of us works through this reality. Having these thoughts means you are exactly where you need to be.

Furthermore, it is easy to admire accomplished consultants and wonder what made them so. What was it that enabled them to write books; speak to audiences around the country; and, even on a rare occasion, get interviewed by a major news organization? If we look only at the end result, we lose sight of the journey that brought them there. That journey had peaks and valleys; mentors; folks who opened doors; opportunities; and, often, a fair bit of luck. There is no doubt that talent is necessary, but that is not the only variable. Getting to know these individuals enables us to humanize their journey and understand that we, too, can follow in their footsteps. Or better yet, maybe a few of you will chart new paths for future generations to follow.

What the Client Wants Versus What the Client Needs

Here is a typical call you will get as a diversity consultant: a potential client contacts you on behalf of an organization grappling with a particular issue relating to an identity group. Perhaps it is a university that is struggling with retaining African American students. A well-intending client may ask, "Can you come in and help us understand this student population and what they need to be successful at our institution?"

There is a significant problem with this question that underlies the very reason why the client absolutely does need you to come in and assist. Implicit in the question is the problematizing of the identity group. Imagine that the client envisions the consultant coming in and giving a presentation on all the things participants should know about Black people and why they are not succeeding. Aside from such a presentation being both simplistic and racist, it also fails to address the issue. A diversity consultant needs to develop the ability to help clients unpack their underlying question while not alienating them. It requires an artful conversation where the diversity consultant offers to create a workshop whereby participants discover and examine the reasons why the organization has not cultivated a culture in which African Americans succeed. Or, even taking a step further, perhaps the organization needs to evaluate how it determined the metrics for success in the first place.

It is a tough spot for diversity consultants to be when clients ask them to do work that ultimately undermines the goals of social justice. But keep in mind that if the clients knew the path forward, they would not be calling us in the first place. We have to give them credit for knowing that they need help. We also need to understand that they may not even know how to phrase the question that articulates their need. But they are on the phone with you, they are willing to be moved, and you just need to get them there.

Wrap-Up

As a diversity consultant, you will have clients who want to know the "right" thing to do that will work in all scenarios. They want a simple solution. Similarly, perhaps there are readers who approached this chapter looking for something parallel: the absolutely "right" path for becoming a diversity consultant. Obviously, in either regard, something that is definitively "right" does not exist. But as a diversity consultant, just as described in this chapter, you will expose people to ideas and points of reflection that they make meaning of in a personal way. We cannot do the hard work for them.

Additionally, in our survey of the field of diversity consultants, we asked participants to give advice to the next generation. The following are some of their responses:

- Be prepared for organizational leaders to agree with the need to develop more equitable practices, but also be ready for many of those same leaders to tell you, "We just don't have the time. . . ."
- Focus. Know what you are good at and share that work with others.
- Find your passion and know the industry in which you wish to work. You must also be clear that a coach, a trainer, a speaker, and a consultant are different things that require different skill sets and competencies. Be clear on what you are, and don't market yourself as something that you are not.
- Understand the difference between social justice education and social justice activism.
- Practice self-care.
- Hire an accountant. . . . *Now!*

Finally, Oscar Wilde (n.d.) wrote, "Be yourself; everyone else is already taken." There are many successful people in this field, and, although it is expected that you will want to emulate facets of what makes them great, outright impersonation is not practical. Authenticity is the greatest tool that diversity educators have at their disposal. The loss of that is the end of your ability to help create positive and lasting social change.

References

Block, P. (2000). *Flawless consulting: A guide to getting your expertise used* (2nd ed.). San Francisco, CA: Jossey-Bass/Pfeiffer.

Box, G. E. P., & Draper, N. R. (1987). *Empirical model-building and response surfaces* (Wiley Series in Probability and Statistics). Hoboken, NJ: Wiley.

Cowman, S. E., & Ferrari, J. R. (2002). "Am I for real?" Predicting impostor tendencies from self-handicapping and affective components. *Social Behavior and Personality: An International Journal, 30*(2), 119–125.

Lorde, A. (2007). *Sister outsider: Essays and speeches by Audre Lorde.* Berkeley, CA: Crossing Press.

Shakespeare, W. (2018). As you like it. In *Medicine and Literature, Volume Two* (pp. 31–93). D.C. Health & Co. Publishers: Boston, MA.

Wilde, O. (n.d.). *Oscar Wilde quotes.* Available from https://www.goodreads .com/quotes/19884-be-yourself-everyone-else-is-already-taken

♦ ♦ ♦ ♦ ♦ ♦

LESSON 7
Effective Listening: The Secret Sauce of Diversity Consultants
John Igwebuike

In more than 25 years of diversity speaking and training, I have learned something important. It may seem neither an earth-shattering piece of professional discovery nor a breakthrough point. It is not guaranteed to drive Web traffic to your site, cause clients to blow up your phone, or multiply your Twitter following. But it has made a tremendous difference in my life personally, professionally, and persistently. What is this idea, you wonder? Six letters: L-I-S-T-E-N. Yes, one of the greatest lessons I have learned in nearly 25 years of work specializing in receptive communication skills is the importance of the art, skill, and science of effective listening.

How might it make a difference for your work? Like most people getting started in this field, I wanted to be a great motivational speaker. I envisioned myself on talk shows, in magazines, and in newspapers. I pictured myself holding crowds in the palm of my hand. In fact, about seven years into speaking, when I was earning enough to help supplement my doctoral studies at The Ohio State University, I took an advanced communication elective as a GPA-booster. I figured I would ace the class, because I was already doing gigs. One project was to prepare a five-minute assignment with an audience activity. One of my classmates prepared a presentation on listening. I thought, "What kind of presentation is that? Everyone does 'listening'!" Yet that was the myth his presentation aimed to debunk—that there is no difference between just hearing and actively listening. He illustrated with two quick exercises, which I missed, along with many others in the class—precisely because I did not L-I-S-T-E-N. I was not focused, silent, and attentive to the speaker.

Though I did ace the course, I was disturbed I had not aced the listening exercises. This gap in my communication repertoire put me on a quest to learn more about the art, skill, and science of effective listening in general and in a diversity context in particular. Thus, were I to give one practical piece of advice to new diversity consultants, it would be "Consider the client."

My clients have run the gamut: a student determined to plan a Black history event at a majority White high school; an inner-city principal who wanted all her students to understand that the United States was globalizing and diversifying; a White grant investigator who wanted to do an African American history program for Black student-athletes in a rural majority private college. In each case, the listening approach was indispensable: Consider the client. What did it take for my clients to bring me to campus? What hoops did they have to hop through to get the funding? What is riding on my performance? What resistance did they face from administration, coworkers, and colleagues? What resistance will they face after I leave? What back-stabbing, microaggressions, cynicism, and arguments did they endure? Through listening, I discovered how my presence might fit in a larger structural or political context: my presentation could impact the funding decision for next year or my ability to sell the power and value of social justice listening could assist the client in future negotiations and engagements. All of these considerations are important.

Consulting, like communication, is a two-way street: there is sender and receiver, speaker and listener. The consultant and client share these roles—one speaks as the other listens; then one listens as the other speaks. The rule of engagement is to enter the relationship all ears, not all open mouth. A consultant cannot know what the client needs unless the consultant L-I-S-T-E-N-S, probes, and reflects. By listening—particularly from the point of view of the *client*—the consultant understands the client's needs, the risks, the culture change sought, the inequities, and so on. A role switch is needed: allow the client to be the expert/consultant. Successful consultants are not just diversity "consultants" but also diversity "listeners."

Prior to that advanced communication course, my considerations would not have been on the client but on me: What suit would I wear? What would I say to make the audience laugh, clap, emote? Which cutting-edge research or theory would dazzle them? How much would I be paid? I-I-I-I-I. Sure, I would call and find out standard information and demographics: time, place, audience, previous speaker, expected outcomes, and so on. However, the focus was on me first, the client second. Contacts only served as a venue for the client to give me information rather than as an opportunity for me to listen—really L-I-S-T-E-N—and learn from this person's point of view.

Thus, the benefits of listening are several. First, to consider the client is to create a space to hear what the *client* has to share: vision, needs, expectations. This process builds trust, as it gives the client the opportunity to unload. This connects to a deep principle of human relations: Everybody wants to be heard. Clients want consultants who not only hear but also listen to understand the context for why the consultant is there. They want to know that they can trust you and be open with you. Every client wants a mutual *relationship*, not just a person who speaks for a while and then collects a check and leaves for the airport. Second, a client who feels understood and who perceives the consultant as receptive and open is more likely to refer the consultant for other speaking opportunities and offer future return engagements. Third, the more the client shares, the more the consultant understands the root cause for engaging with the consultant. This is an opportunity to decline the engagement if there is little alignment between the organization and the consultant's work. Fourth, a diversity consultant who comes to hear the stories and understand the context from the client is better able to target the presentation closer to the client's expectations while staying true to the consultant's own message. Being patient enough to listen to and understand the client's multiple competing factors can add nuanced vigor and credible power to the presentation. The presentation that considers the client allows cocreative transformation to occur.

Martin Luther King Jr. (1966) presciently wrote, "A riot is the language of the unheard." Regardless of background, experiences, and preferences, everyone wants to be heard. Indeed, I find it unsurprising that the founder of modern psychology, William James, noted that the deepest craving of the human soul is to be understood. Just as everyone wants to eat, so too does everyone want to be heard. Diversity clients are no different; therefore, consider the client and L-I-S-T-E-N.

Reference

King, M. L. (1967, April 14). The other America [Transcript]. Available from https://www.crmvet.org/docs/otheram.htm.

◆ ◆ ◆ ◆ ◆ ◆

LESSON 8
There's a Black Man Talking!
Bryant K. Smith

A good friend of mine, Lee Jones, gave me my first professional speaking job when he was unable to fly out of his home airport. Jones was a prolific speaker who used to tell a story about speaking to some educators, relating that he asked them, "What's the first thing you noticed when I walked out onto the stage?"

Someone in the audience yelled out, "You have a nice suit jacket on," which Jones then proceeded to remove and followed up with, "Now what is the first thing you notice?"

Another audience member replied, "Your tie . . . you have a very nice tie," which Jones quickly removed. According to Jones, this back-and-forth banter about what was the first thing his audience noticed went on until he had removed his shoes and belt on stage. Finally, the provost at the institution stood up and said to his fellow faculty members, "You all are embarrassing us; if you don't admit what we all know to be true—that the first thing we noticed was that Dr. Jones is a Black man—he will be standing on the stage naked momentarily."

That story, along with a few others Jones has shared, has always resonated with me, and it has impacted the way I approach my work as a diversity practitioner. That story and the lessons within it have done more to prepare me to engage my audiences than any class, book, or theory.

Lesson number one from Jones's story: Prepare to be visible and invisible at the same time when doing this work. I am a dark-complected

American man of African descent. My melanin count is high, and whenever I walk into a space or onto a stage or into a classroom it is clear that a Black man is walking in and occupying that space. People see me and register me as a Black man in their minds, whatever that may mean to them. However, it is how they define my Blackness in their minds that also makes me invisible to them. All of a sudden people see me as Black but refuse to see color at the same time.

W. E. B. Du Bois said it best when he stated in *The Souls of Black Folk*, "It is a peculiar sensation, this double-consciousness, this sense of always looking at one's self through the eyes of others, of measuring one's soul by the tape of a world that looks on in amused contempt and pity" (quoted in Foner, 1950, p. 437). I would say there is a triple consciousness, because in many audiences there is a fear that goes along with their contempt and pity when they see that a Black man is in charge of their training. How do you prepare yourself to discuss difference when at the same time you know if you discuss your own racial difference it will make the audience uncomfortable to the point that they may actually shut down, ignore you, not participate in the session, and ultimately write a poor evaluation—which could then result in missing additional business or recommendations? In short, how do you promote yourself as an expert to an audience who sees but does not want to acknowledge all of you, especially when seeing all of a person is the basis for our interaction during that time?

Lesson number two: Your audience is not on your side at first; they don't know, like, or trust you. As a Black male presenter you come to the venue carrying baggage that you didn't pack. You may be the first Black man in a positive position of power that many in your audience have ever seen. You may be the most educated example of a Black man they have ever encountered. You may be the first Black man they have seen who was not on television, playing sports, or entertaining them. You may be the first Black man they have seen who was not wearing handcuffs or an orange jumpsuit or depicted in a mug shot.

You stand there draped in your Blackness, and all they see is a person who has come to attack everything White. You have come to give them a history lesson on slavery and the evils of Whiteness as personified by White men. Your very presence as a Black man is powerful enough to evoke traumatic memories of White guilt and privilege, and the only way they can escape their feelings is to invalidate you, your expertise, and your manhood. In the audience there may be people who have seen you before and value your expertise, but some don't want to be there and don't care about you. There may be one or two audience members or event planners present who know and like you and who are responsible for getting you the job. However, as a Black man, speaker, and trainer, what makes this different for me is it becomes my job to reduce and eliminate the audience's defenses, and I don't have a lot of time to do it. Lee Jones, by addressing the elephant in the room at the beginning of his speech, was able to remove his audience's defenses, gain their trust, and demonstrate his expertise with a few simple questions. He simultaneously demonstrated why there was a need for him to be there, declared his expertise, and made everyone comfortable with being uncomfortable. He managed to do all of those things and remain authentically Black.

Lesson number three: always speak truth to power. There is nothing more demanding than the truth. Frederick Douglass said:

> If there is no struggle, there is no progress. Those who profess to favor freedom and yet depreciate agitation, are men who want crops without plowing up the ground. They want rain without thunder and lightning. They want the ocean without the awful roar of its many waters. This struggle may be a moral one; or it may be a physical one; or it may be both moral and physical; but it must be a struggle. Power concedes nothing without a demand. It never did and it never will. (quoted in Du Bois, 2003, p. 5)

The truth requires something from those who speak it and those who hear it, and that is why it is so demanding and powerful. There are many Black male speakers who do diversity work, and there are many of them who do what I call *cooning* and *fluff*. Their approach to diversity training is to deal only with the superficial—those things that would be fun and not offensive to anyone (primarily White people) in their audience. They care more about being invited back than they do about making significant progress. They would rather be liked than respected. They offer their clients progress without struggle, whereas Jones, with his short story and a simple question, was able to demonstrate that, like Frederick Douglass, struggling in search of progress is a noble and honorable undertaking. Through his example I learned early on that it would be better for me to sit quietly in my house being a Black man than to speak on stage disguised as someone else. At some point in this business as a Black man, you are going to have to ask yourself, "What does integrity mean to me?"

It does not matter whether you call it "selling out" or "buying in"; it is still representing yourself as something other than what you are. Learning to be comfortable as a Black man is paramount to my success in this business. I had to learn to be okay with being the only Black man in some spaces. I had to be okay with being the first Black man in some spaces. I had to understand the need for Black men to show up, show out, stand up, and speak up in the spaces that need diversity training, because to do anything other than that was counterproductive.

In the end, this work is about helping people to see others as they want to be seen, not as you want to see them. In some ways it is therapeutic to walk on stage or into a room and be the most authentic representation of a Black man that I can be. For 60 minutes, 90 minutes, a half day, a full day, or an entire retreat, I am able to showcase Black male excellence to a group of people who before interacting with me thought the phrase "Black male excellence" was oxymoronic. When I do my job right, audience members, regardless of race or gender, walk away having learned and having grown as a result of our interaction. I have added value to their lives and put purpose to my own life at the same time.

No matter how tense or frustrating that time we spend together is, I generally feel empowered, because I understand the value of my ability to help the audience wrestle with the complexities of racial and other differences. I know that my perspective is rooted in my identity and experiences as a Black man living in the United States of America. Nonetheless, sometimes I just want to yell out in the middle of a training, "Shut up and listen, there's a Black man talking!" However, there is no need for me to do so. Yelling would just add more noise to the room. Like Jones, I don't want or need to add more noise to the room. I am there to add clarity, wisdom, and understanding. The reason I enjoy my work so much is because I have found a way to reduce the noise that surrounds me as a Black man. I have found a way to give a voice to Black men and other voiceless people by amplifying the similarities we share through our humanity. It is not easy work, but it is necessary and extremely gratifying when done correctly. In the end, I never have to yell that there is a Black man talking. I just have to help the audience remove the noise in their lives that kept them from acknowledging what it was that they were truly hearing and seeing, before we all find ourselves standing on the stage naked and embarrassed.

References

Du Bois, W. E. B. (2003). *The souls of Black folk*. New York, NY: Random House.

Foner, P. S. (Ed.). (1950). *The life and writings of Frederick Douglass* (Vol. 2). New York, NY: International Publishers.

◆ ◆ ◆ ◆ ◆ ◆

LESSON 9
White Man Talking
Tim Wise

First off, I guess I should note that I don't really fashion myself a diversity consultant. Rather, I'm an antiracism educator, and for me this is an important distinction, because diversity consulting is an incredibly broad and often vague category. So although it includes people who do serious antioppression and antiracism work, it also encompasses folks who just try to help everyone get along or manage crisis situations rather than create more equitable institutional structures.

That said, and in whatever capacity a White person is trying to do this kind of work, there are certain things I think we need to keep in mind.

Lesson One: Have a Sense of Humility

When White folks do equity and diversity work, there is more that we *don't* know than that which we do know. That's connected to being White, because we haven't been the direct targets of racism. We haven't been required as a condition of survival to learn about these things the way people of color have. So we need to be humble and recognize that people of color in our classrooms, workshops, and audiences know just as much if not more than we do. If we understand that, we can create an environment where we learn from each other. But if we forget that, the experience can become very colonial and implicitly feed the notion that the "White expert" is the one with the broadest base of knowledge.

Lesson Two: Be Transparent

White people in this work can't talk about privilege or internalized bias or subconscious bias in others unless we're willing to be transparent about our own privileges and biases. If we want to elicit recognition from someone about a subject as emotionally fraught as privilege or bias, we have to own those things in ourselves. Otherwise, we're not going to be very effective. No one wants to be lectured about one of their failings by someone who isn't willing to acknowledge also being part of the problem. But when we own our personal biases and privileges, it becomes less frightening for the folks we're working with to own theirs and move forward toward challenging both.

Lesson Three: Have a Sense of History

Those of us who are White need to have an understanding that we are part of a long tradition of solidarity and White allyship. Having a sense of history is important, because if you don't understand this tradition, it becomes easy to think that you're special and that you discovered some truth no other White person has ever understood. That's dangerous because it contributes to a savior mentality that elevates you above the folks of color who have always understood these things. It also cuts you off from an important tradition within the White community from which you can learn. If I don't know that history, I can't as easily learn from the mistakes of previous allies and people who worked in solidarity. I have to understand the history so I can learn from it, both the good and the bad.

Lesson Four: Be Accountable

For White people doing this work, the ultimate risk is not ours. People of color are the ones who have the most to lose if our work goes badly. Therefore, it's people of color whose lead we should follow in this work. We need to pay attention to the issues they're most focused on in a given institutional setting and lend our support in those specific areas, rather than simply assuming we know what the real issues are. As an example, this might mean that although our inclination is to jump into a conversation about subconscious bias, people of color in a given organizational setting might be struggling with *overt* and conscious racism or structural racism that operates at a deeper level than the interpersonal. If we aren't listening to folks of color but are just going with the focus we prefer, we're not being accountable to the people most at risk.

Lesson Five: Be Hard on Systems but Soft on People

Essentially this means showing empathy to people who are struggling with the concepts we're trying to explain and offer to them, recognizing the systematic roots of their resistance. This is often difficult because when White folks reach a certain level of so-called wokeness, there is a tendency to be judgmental about those who are less so. But empathy is important, because whatever it is you're hoping other folks will "get" is something you didn't always understand either. Judging someone on Friday for something you only came to see on Monday, figuratively speaking, is arrogant and ultimately unhelpful. In my experience, empathy works better. People who express messed-up ideas about race and gender and sexuality and other things express those ideas in large measure because they have been conditioned to do so in a system of profound inequality. So for me to be hard on them as people and not show empathy is to overindividualize the problem and ignore the systemic nature of it. By being soft on people—even those who are really messed up—and being hard on systems, I am addressing inequality at the root. I am also doing something that allows people to show empathy for me because there are going to be times when I screw up, and if I want empathy, I have to be willing to extend it.

Lesson Six: Be Open to Pushback

It is essential not to get defensive about pushback, whether it is from a person of color or from another person who is White. I have to remember this work is dialogic in nature, not a monologue. Part of that is the give-and-take that comes from being challenged on certain issues. I need to be prepared and open and try to think through the various parts of pushback I might get to become better at responding in a way that is impactful and helpful and moves the conversation forward.

Lesson Seven: Be Flexible in Your Approach

This took a long time for me to learn. Being flexible means being prepared to give up certain long-held maxims, theories, or concepts, at least in the moment, to bring people to where I need them to be. So, for instance, often when we ask White folks to address White privilege, they raise issues of their marginalization as women or as lesbian, gay, bisexual, transgender, and queer/questioning (LGBTQ) folks or on the basis of class status, often as a deflection technique. Once I would have responded to such a thing harshly, probably calling it out as a hijacking move and insisting that we focus on race and Whiteness exclusively. But what I have learned over the years is that even if that maneuver *is* intended as a deflection, it's far more helpful to let whoever is using that tactic to have his or her little victory for a few minutes. If I'm willing to give the person a few minutes to acknowledge how horrible the pain of sexism, straight supremacy, or economic marginality is, and then use that as a way to connect to the conversation about race (because, after all, these things are interconnected in many ways), then I can bring that person closer to where I need him or her to be without letting the conversation become derailed.

For instance, in the face of that kind of deflection, simply to acknowledge how painful those other forms of oppression are and to note how painful it is when others deny those realities or make light of them can help the person who raised these other issues see how hurtful it is for people of color when White folks do the same about racist injury and White privilege. By allowing folks the space to name their pain but then connecting it back to the pain we're focusing on for a particular session, we can keep the conversation moving and build empathy and solidarity. Shutting it down, as I would have done in the old days, only builds walls of resentment and defensiveness.

Lesson Eight: Be in Collaboration Rather Than Competition

This was also hard for me to learn in some regards. Early in this work I came from an unhealthy and competitive place where I felt as though I needed to know more, do more, and be more impactful than other White people in the work. It wasn't always conscious, but I think I felt a need to be *the* leading White antiracist or some such thing. I didn't feel in competition with people of color, because I knew they were the ones who needed to lead the work whereas Whites needed to follow their lead. But within the White space there was definitely a competitiveness that was totally screwed up (and very, very White, truth be told). What I've come to appreciate is that even though there are Whites in the work who have different approaches from mine (and with whom I might have rather profound disagreements), unless I think of this as a collaborative effort where we're all trying to get somewhere together, I end up in an unhealthy place where it becomes a contest between different folks instead of us being on the same team. If I don't keep that in mind, I become the person who is just trying to beat them for the next conference contract or speaking gig rather than trying to figure out how we can better collaborate by helping to inform each other's work in a more productive way.

◆ ◆ ◆ ◆ ◆ ◆

LESSON 10
Be Prepared for Anything and Surprised by Nothing
Vernon A. Wall

I feel blessed for many reasons. One is that I am able to be in settings where I can encourage "courageous conversations" about social justice and inclusion issues. Another is that I stand on the shoulders of amazing mentors and teachers who came before me. I am in debt to those individuals who nurtured me and continue to encourage me in this work. In this vein, I'd like to share six reflections on consulting with the theme "Be prepared for anything and surprised by nothing," a philosophy that has guided me along my journey.

1. *Get an accountant—NOW!* I have this as number one because this is the first thing that consultants typically overlook. U.S. tax law affects consultants differently, and there are nuances based on state law. A good accountant will work on your behalf to help you navigate your finances.

2. *Fellow consultants are partners in this work, not competition.* We need more of us doing this work. As a result, it is my duty to encourage others on their journey. We can learn from each other and impact our communities in powerful ways. Recommending other consultants for work shows that you recognize others' strengths.

3. *Focus.* There is no need for you to be a one-stop shop. I know what I am good at. I also know when to say no to an ask. Although I want to be of service to as many organizations and/or campuses as I can be, I also know that others may have a greater impact based on the topic or the environment.

4. *Publish!* In order to be respected as a consultant (specifically in higher education), you must write. Blogs. Articles. Book chapters. Videos. Presentations for conferences. The goal is to establish yourself as an "expert" in your subject and content. Your visibility is vital to your success.

5. *Intake conversations are crucial.* Getting a sense for your client's needs and the audience you are spending time with is essential. Do your homework. Check out websites. Read mission statements and other relevant documents. Add special touches to your handouts and presentations to illustrate that you have done some research.

6. *Don't forget your own personal development.* Attend conference presentations to enhance your learning. Continue to read scholarly work in your area. This enables you to remain current.

Always remember, the work that we do makes a profound difference to this generation and to generations to come. Our mission is important. Let's all work to show up as our authentic selves in connecting and healing ways.

4

Putting Out Your Shingle

Eddie Moore Jr., Art Munin, and Marguerite Penick-Parks

Preparation is the key to any good recipe. You have to do prep work before starting to cook. Leaving something out because you are too tired to run to the store to collect all of the ingredients leads to an incomplete recipe that is not as well received by your audience. It is the same with being a diversity consultant. Before you even think about contracting out for your very first gig, there are many things you must have in place. This chapter is about what you need to have in place as you take your first steps into this field and what some of your next steps are once you get started. Many of the lessons and tips come from the mistakes of those who came before you. Get these items ready and lay them out for consistency, clarity, and brand. If some of these recommendations sound simplistic, they probably are, and if you have five or six consulting opportunities annually, tracking this information may be easy. But the busier you get, the more being prepared up front will save you in time, energy, and potential lost opportunities because of missteps.

What Is Your Special Sauce?

When you think of your brand—your special sauce—what is it that makes you stand out? We recommend that you create one workshop that is your signature presentation—the one only you can do. From there you start to build your brand. With that workshop in mind, you then need to start with a name. The name should quickly let an organization know what it will get if it hires you. If you say you are a diversity consultant, that only gives the organization the main ingredient. Do you teach skills, do you help set goals, are you limited to K–12 or postsecondary education? Do you focus on general "diversity" work, or are you based in issues of social justice and accustomed to confront participants on their power and White privilege? Your brand needs to include not only your unique, creative name but also your mission and your vision. Those can be in the byline, but they must be clear and concise. The following is a good, clear example: The Privilege Institute: Making it REAL—Research, Education, Action, Leadership (The Privilege Institute, 2017).

People who read this slogan know the four main ingredients that The Privilege Institute offers. It is important to be this clear and focused. Do not be too creative or artsy if it distracts from your message. Stay away from current or trendy slogans, because you do not want to have to redo it in five years when that slogan is outdated. When in doubt, keep it simple; you do not want to have to explain yourself.

Price

It is important to have a pricing scale. You want to be certain you fit into multiple price points, especially when you are starting out. One of the authors of this chapter (Moore) has a motto of "Affordable, Available, Negotiable." Another author (Munin) always includes the following statement in every proposal:

> I value my workshops at [dollar amount] plus flight and hotel. I also will e-mail you the packet ahead of time so that you could make as many copies as you see fit. This is typically cheaper than me making the copies and adding that cost to the deal. But, I do hold true to the business philosophy I have published on the front page of my website. My central purpose in starting this consulting company was not just to make a profit. I was looking to expand my opportunities to advocate for social justice. Therefore, if this price is outside of the confines of your budget, please talk to me. It is never my desire to turn down a worthwhile educational opportunity, like this one, over money.

As a consultant you have to decide what is worth your time to do. Is the gig about making connections versus making money? You are the only one who can answer that question, but for each consulting opportunity consider the following:

- Can I afford to do this gig for any amount? Are the networking opportunities worth taking less money, or is the learning opportunity more essential than the cost?
- How much time will it take for me to prepare for this contract?
- Are travel costs included in the remuneration or separate?
- Am I willing to reduce the costs, and if so, how much can I reduce while still making it worth my time?
- Are there other ways to make this trip worthwhile?
- What value do I place on my time?

We also recommend you consider how to be economical by scheduling more than one event in an area at the same time. Two positives come from this approach: one, you are reducing your carbon footprint by combining travel, and two, you may also help multiple organizations be able to afford you by enabling them to share the cost of your travel.

Last, you will need to consider what type of organization is booking you when considering your price. A small not-for-profit may have different budgetary constraints than a large university or a business. You may want to take into account that some public institutions can have state restraints on funding. You will want to work within their guidelines, especially if there is a cap that calls for a bid as opposed to an offer. The right amount for a contract reflects the value of your time and what an organization will pay.

Website Creation

Before designing your page, review dozens of diversity consultant websites to see what you like and do not like and what you can pull in to your own unique brand. Your website is your portal to the world. For people who do not know you, this is the resource they use to determine whether or not they want to partner with you, so it is crucial to present a professional face to potential partners. Consider the following points:

- Who is going to build and maintain the website? Unless you have those skills, you will need help to design it, keep it upgraded, and maintain its elements so it does not become outdated or stale.
- Be concise and creative; utilize color, pictures, videos, and any other creative elements that might engage viewers.
- Include testimonials, references, social media access points/options, a biography, or consider a curriculum vitae or resumé, depending on your field.
- When selecting a Web host, ask what analytical reports they provide so you can track who visits your website and where they are located.
- Be certain the weblink is short and concise and can be utilized in all of your promotional materials, including e-mails.
- Incorporate your brand into everything you do. Be consistent in color, style, and vision.
- When selecting the e-mail account for your business, use one that is separate from any other positions you may hold, so you will always have that e-mail, regardless of where your career or life takes you.

Business Cards

Again, one of the most important things you should do is look at all of the cards you have collected. Look for elements you like and those you do not. Which cards do you keep? What drew you to those particular cards?

One of the most common mistakes people make with business cards is putting too much information on them. Make sure that recipients know who you are, what you can do for them, and how they can contact you. Beyond these three key points, keep it simple, stick with your color schemes and your brand, and make it professional and creative without being too busy.

Outreach Through Social Media

Outreach is essential to putting your name into the field and keeping it out there. With the increase in technology over the years, creating and maintaining outreach is key. One approach we recommend is that for the first few years hire what we call a "hustle coach." A hustle coach is someone who can guide you through the creation and launch of your social media presence as well as your consulting endeavor. Another recommendation is to get everything prepared—website, newsletter, flyers, Facebook, Twitter—before even starting. Set a launch date for your consulting business when all of your messaging goes up and out on the same day.

As you build your business, social media can be an incredibly valuable tool to not only reach clients but also maintain connections, foster collaborations, share resources, and build community. However, as many of us know, social media can also come with negative repercussions if used unwisely.

At its best, social media is an effective way to connect with individuals and groups who may have interest in what you offer through your diversity consulting. You must employ social media with a strategy in mind. This is not simply your personal Facebook account; you are a business—you have a brand, name, website, and reputation. Everything you do on social media must be consistent and professional:

- Share pictures of your bookings that highlight the organizations that brought you in, rather than simply self-promoting.
- Create a hashtag for each booking and encourage participants to live-tweet during your session. This may foster connections among the participants and enable you to look back later at what resonated.
- Decide whether or not to create a social media presence separate from your personal social media. There is no right or wrong answer to this question. It comes down to how closely you wish to blend the varying dimensions of your life.
- Share yourself. This is an opportunity for potential clients to get to know you personally. They will value seeing who you are, what you are involved in, and how you engage with others.
- Diversity and social justice work is complicated and multifaceted. Think critically about what you choose to post, share, or comment. When in doubt, talk to someone offline to get another opinion. Remember, in this digital age, anything you post can (and will) return to you.

- To attract attention, be creative and fun. Again, tie it all to your brand.
- If you have access to interns, use them!
- Be consistent and thought-provoking in your professional posts so viewers will return to hear more. Remember, this is your portal to the field. Potential clients may initially find out about you on social media. What is the first impression you want to make?

Unfortunately, we have all seen instances of social media going awry. Avoid the following pitfalls:

- Keep personal posts to a minimum or within your friend group.
- Watch for hate groups or attacks in the comments section. Choose social media platforms that allow you to block accounts.
- Remember that there are times to use more traditional forms of media. People still listen to the radio and read newsletters, so be certain that you are not focusing all of your efforts on social media.
- Last, if you make a mistake on social media, own up to it, apologize, seek to make amends, and move on. Simply deleting your post, refusing to comment, and hoping it will go away will not work. This is an opportunity for you to exemplify how to own a mistake with dignity. A public error demands a public accounting.

Testimonials

Testimonials are a true and honest advertisement from people who have participated in your bookings. They are an invaluable resource to you as a consultant, because these individuals are agreeing to vouch for you and your work, and future clients may regard those testimonials as crucial when considering your services. Consider the following ways to maximize this approach:

- Always follow up after a session to ask for a testimonial; make it a habit.
- Consider including pictures with testimonials. Ideally this picture will be of you with the person giving the testimonial.

This will personalize the words and make it more likely that people will read them.

- Highlight diverse people and organizations in the pictures and testimonials.
- Focus on testimonials that speak to content, presentation style, and outcomes.

Financial Planning

To reiterate the advice from one of the consultants in this book, the first thing you need to do is hire an accountant. Being in legal compliance is essential; we cannot emphasize these words enough. Hire an accountant, be certain you understand your legal and financial responsibilities, and keep very detailed and accurate records. If you forget to report one consulting gig, the IRS might flag you. Keep in mind the saying "You can do it right a thousand times, but you only get to do it wrong once." That one mistake can be costly in terms of finances and personal energy expended.

We also encourage you to explore incorporating as a limited liability company (LLC). It is not our place to advise you one way or another, because the decision is unique to your circumstances as a consultant. The decision becomes even more important if you decide to do this work full-time. Regardless, a financial planner and/or a lawyer are the best professionals to give you advice on this point.

The last piece on financial planning we offer is to be strategic about your expenditures. It is worthwhile to use credit cards that earn points and to enroll in airline and hotel rewards programs, as those benefits can accrue quickly and be used to offset consulting expenses. Or better yet, they can be a vacation reward to help maintain your personal health and wellness in this difficult work.

Contracts

Contracts are absolutely necessary in this work to not only detail your remuneration but also outline the expectations of the agreed-upon consulting work. Care and attention to this document on the front end can prevent trouble down the road.

For some clients this process will be easy, because they will require that you utilize their organization's contract. This is often the case if you work with any government entity (school, university, municipality). As part of their process, they may also require you to register as a vendor in the state vendor system. Typically these processes are not difficult but do prolong the time it takes to finalize the contract.

For times when an organization does not have a standard contract, you should be prepared with a template of your own, which includes the following information:

- *Services provided.* Include the title of a presentation, amount of preparation time needed, amount of time allotted (e.g., two-hour workshop), and type of service (e.g., interactive workshop, keynote, program review).
- *Remuneration.* Include a description of when and how payment will be delivered. Examples are at time of presentation or to be mailed after services are rendered. Also, be clear about reimbursing expenses if the client is covering travel, lodging, and/or meals.
- *Designation of duties.* Identify the person at the organization with whom you will work to finalize the presentation.
- *Contract cancellation.* Detail the options for termination of services, associated time lines, and potential costs in case of termination.
- *Copyright.* Include a statement on copyright for the consulting materials you provide through the course of this contract (e.g., PowerPoints, worksheets, handouts).
- *Signature lines.* Ensure that each signature area includes a line for the name to be printed, along with the date.

Our last pieces of advice are to read everything you are signing and consider consulting an attorney for advice and clarification. A mistake with a contract can impact not only your booking but also your reputation. Furthermore, keep copies of everything. Consult with your attorney and/or financial planner on how long you should keep records. Finally, guard your personal information (e.g., social security number) so it does not become public. If you e-mail a contract or W-9 form, be certain you know the recipient.

Learning Outcomes and Evaluation

When creating diversity consulting proposals, invoices, or contracts, some groups may require you to submit learning outcomes. Even if they do not ask, we recommend that you include them. Without learning outcomes, it is difficult to assess the quality of the consultation and the results achieved.

Once you determine your learning outcomes, create a standard evaluation form tied to them, one that is easy to modify so you do not have to start from scratch every time. In creating your evaluation, try to strike a balance between assessing how participants felt about the experience and what they gained from their time working with you. Both can be important pieces of information. However, we have seen examples of evaluations that rely too much on how participants felt about the workshop. Knowing that people really appreciated and valued the experience is helpful only if we also know how it might positively impact their organization.

Last, we want to include a word of caution on pre-/postevaluations for diversity consultant contracts. Although this assessment method can be helpful in a number of fields, it can be problematic in diversity consulting. For example, one of the authors of this book (Munin) conducted an evaluation for a diversity presentation. After analyzing the exit survey, he discovered that following the workshop most participants responded that they felt less prepared to navigate dialogue relating to diversity and social justice. Munin failed to account for the fact that on a presurvey participants will sometimes inflate their beliefs regarding their comfort or knowledge relating to these topics. Then, when the workshop exposes their lack of familiarity or discomfort, the ratings go down for the postsurvey. With this caveat in mind, an evaluation does help the consultant to analyze aspects of the presentation. However, you may not want to put yourself in such a position with a client at the end of a contract.

Handouts/Presentations

In order to save time, make templates of your presentations that are easily modified for different organizations and audiences. Most consultants will have three or four presentations they generally do. These may be keynotes or workshops, so you may want to prepare a different length version of each—for example, a three-hour presentation and a one-hour version. The more work you do up front, the less you need to do as you go on:

- Make a separate file of handouts for each presentation, and make them as clear as possible the first time so you do not have to keep redoing them.
- Give credit where credit is due. Cite research or other consultants' work.
- Use clear and engaging visual aids.
- Ensure that handouts and slides use font sizes and typefaces that are accessible and readable for all, including viewers who are color blind.
- Remember to include subtitles in video clips.
- Prepare materials before you arrive. Many organizations will want both the presentation and the handouts in advance. The more organized you keep them, the easier they are to share.
- Consider sustainability by sharing the handouts electronically via e-mail or a conference app.
- Include collaborative or hands-on activities to engage participants and get them talking.
- Summarize large sections of text in handouts or presentations rather than reading them aloud.
- Provide ample time for participants to access the material if your handouts are long enough that they need to be read prior to the session in order to convey your information.
- Build in time to work with attendees to develop an action plan, a list of goals, or something similar so that they can continue the work.

Scheduling

As a consultant, you are the only one who can decide what you can handle and what you should turn down, how long you want your sessions scheduled for, and how often you can be available for work. Often people starting out feel that they should take every opportunity offered.

However, what if you have a full-time job? How much time can you be away before it conflicts with your job responsibilities? Or if you are attempting to do this full-time, how much do you need to cover your financial needs while maintaining a healthy savings account? Before you start the process, we once again recommend you think through these issues, set a budget, and determine what you need and what you can do. Overextending yourself can lead to underdelivering on your consulting contracts.

In addition to thinking about how many gigs you are able to do, think about what the best length is for the information you want to share. You can always do more, but it is essential to know first what you are able to do and what you need to do and then grow from there.

Concerning the general timing of talks, the following are good general rules:

- Keynotes should be a minimum of 60 minutes (40–45 minutes to talk and 15–20 minutes for questions).
- Workshops should be a minimum of 2 hours. They can also be a half day (3–4 hours) or a full day (6–8 hours).

Dress/Wardrobe

How you present yourself tells the story of you as a professional. As you plan your business cards, your website, your social media, and your presentation content, you are considering the image you want to embody. Your wardrobe does the same thing; clothing and accessories are an opportunity to express your identity, so determine your appearance with care. There is not a right or wrong, but there is a "who you are," so take that into account. Recommendations from those in the field include the following:

- Choose your clothing carefully, considering what travels well.
- Avoid logos or images because of their potential cultural impact.
- Demonstrate respect for your audience by dressing professionally and avoiding business casual unless you deem it appropriate for the venue.

Take Care of Yourself!

As the saying goes, this is a marathon, not a sprint. We need diversity consultants out in the world doing good work over the long haul. In order to do that, you cannot ignore your personal health and wellness. Take care of yourself, because it is the right thing to do. However, if you need external motivation, do it because you are a leader—an example others will look up to in the future. Consider the following key points:

- Give yourself time to rest and recover.
- Traveling is hard on your body over time. Be mindful about the way you eat, sleep, and exercise on the road. Travel with a noise machine. Every hotel sounds different, and having that consistent background noise can be a big help.
- If you are a part-time consultant, balance it with your full-time job. Be fair and clear about your expectations with your employer.
- Know when to ask for help; then ask for it. Use the network of support you have established.
- You do not need to be all things to all people all the time. If you are struggling to maintain balance, pretend for a moment that someone you love is in the predicament you find yourself. Reflect on what advice you would give that person. At times, we will respond with more kindness and compassion to those we love than we do to ourselves. Everyone deserves flexibility and grace, especially you.

Thank You!

Always remember to write and send thank-you notes. Some people believe an e-mail is adequate, and although e-mail is better than nothing, a personal touch in the form of a handwritten note at the end of a consulting contract can go a long way toward encouraging referrals or a return trip. One of the authors (Munin) also often sends a diversity or social justice book to the individual in charge of his contract, to both share a resource and strengthen the connection.

Reference

The Privilege Institute. (2017). *Home.* Available from https://www.the privilegeinstitute.com/

◆ ◆ ◆ ◆ ◆ ◆

LESSON 11
Stress Kills

Sumun L. Pendakur

Just this spring, I was walking the tightrope of juggling a fairly new and exciting job with a number of high-profile keynoting, consulting, and facilitation gigs. To add another element to the mix, I was early in my pregnancy, often collapsing with exhaustion when I got home in the evening. However, life does not stop, and my husband and my five-year-old son needed me (especially to find that *one* missing Lego!). My body was full of adrenaline and fatigue, seemingly all the time, as I pinballed from one deadline to another.

One day, I traveled via Amtrak to deliver a keynote for Asian Pacific American Heritage Month for a campus that was struggling to serve its Asian American and Pacific Islander students in meaningful and community-oriented ways. By evening, it was showtime, and I poured my heart and intellect into offering an hourlong personal and political talk, followed by an open question-and-answer (Q&A) session. I fielded deeply emotional questions from the attendees for the Q&A, where I chose to be raw and vulnerable, and many audience members were in tears. I held space for their emotions and needs, and when that portion was done, almost 20 people lined up to talk to me. They revealed mental health concerns, feelings of alienation, desires to explore facets of identity more deeply, stories of feeling marginalized by the institution and silenced by peers, and more. I talked with each person, hugging each one when we came to closure, and made room for the next. I felt utterly drained and strangely elated when the evening finally came to a close hours later, in a way I think is unique to practitioners engaged in social justice education and diversity consulting. For those of us for whom this work is a calling and part of a personal equity mission, the story of this keynote experience is but one example of the tremendous emotional labor that goes into doing the work with heart and rigorous attention to justice.

Against the backdrop of seemingly unceasing systemic and structural injustice, the struggle to find balance, sustain oneself for the long haul, maintain integrity, and make space for the learning, growth, demands, and needs of clients/participants is real. One quote exemplifies the particular stress and strain for me: "In the battle to maintain dignity, self-respect, and legitimacy, many diversity workers experience a fatigue that leads to illness, depression, isolation, and exclusion" (Fasching-Varner, Albert, Mitchell, & Allen, 2015, p. xvii).

You are carrying not only your own (often traumatic) experiences and fatigue but also the heartrending stories that people tell you, as well as your knowledge of institutional failure to support those on the margins. You are faced with the looming dangers of falling off the precipice of exhaustion or losing sight of the goal of always centering those who experience marginalization and minoritization. Maintaining your personal health and wellness must be a priority.

Tenets for Praxis

Over the years I have engaged in this work (inside multiple institutions and as a consultant), I have found the following five tenets invaluable to my praxis. I hope they will be helpful to you, as you consider your desires to engage in this work with authenticity over the long road ahead.

Value Yourself

No one will take care of you like you will. Functioning well in a White supremacist, capitalist state takes emotional and psychological resources, so identify what keeps you whole and feeling like you matter. Is being fairly compensated essential to your sense of self-worth? Learn how to negotiate, and do not be afraid to aim high (as long as your work is also high quality!). Do you find yourself often rundown and getting sick? You cannot help anyone if your own oxygen mask is not on first. Purposeful self-care is not only essential for the survival of the diversity consultant but also important role modeling for those around us. Do you feel pressure to take gigs (whether or not you want to) because you are afraid the work will evaporate? Then name that for yourself and do not be afraid to set boundaries with your time. If you are good at what you do, opportunities will continue to present themselves—do not say "Yes" out of a sense of desperation.

Learn How to Say "No"

Speaking of setting boundaries, learning how to say "No" has been a journey for me. Many others share this challenge, as well. However, saying "No" is one of the most empowering things we can do—and I say this particularly as a woman of color who often carries multiple burdens and expectations in various spaces. The critical part of learning how to say no is that we are actually making intentional space to say "Yes" to the opportunities that truly speak to us, opening ourselves to the gigs that leverage our gifts and talents in worthwhile ways and ensuring our longevity in this type of work, because we have not fallen into the abyss of burnout and cynicism.

Maintain Your Integrity

None of this work means anything if you have lost sight of the reasons you started in the first place: to be a change agent, to empower others, to inspire social justice–oriented action. For example, if you find yourself centering the needs and comfort of the majority over those experiencing minoritization, you have veered from the path of equity-minded transformation. Being willing to examine and critique yourself is not only a central point of cultural humility; it is also a necessity to maintain integrity, authenticity, and a moral compass—all of which are essential to doing this work in a way that does no harm to communities already marginalized.

Identify Your Call-In Crew

Who pulls you back from the edge—the edge of exhaustion, the edge of sliding down a slippery slope of shoddy diversity and inclusion work, the edge of giving up? Identify a few trusted friends or family members who will hold you accountable to the goals you have set for yourself, your health, and your practice. My husband, for example, sees my work, knows my fears, and calls me in when he needs to, so that I am not facing the road ahead alone. We can feel isolated and alienated in and by this work, so asking others to hold you account-able to your stated intentions is paramount to your survival and success.

Find the Joy

Finally, and possibly most importantly, find and claim your sources of joy. What lifts you and brings you happiness? Contentment? Laughter? I laugh loud and often, because laughter is not only a form of resis-tance but also healing for the cracks in my spirit. Your joy can lift oth-ers—because our work of crafting the beloved community should not be approached from a space of toxicity, negativity, or fear. My joy gets me up each day, ready to do battle again, in a compassionately critical way, because we are lucky to hold the stories and hopes of those we work with and for. My hope for you is that you approach your role as a diversity consultant knowing the costs associated with the work and yet choosing to engage this field with your own tenets of meaningful and sustainable praxis to guide you.

Reference

Fasching-Varner, K. J., Albert, K. A., Mitchell, R. W., & Allen, C. M. (2015). *Racial battle fatigue in higher education: Exposing the myth of post-racial America*. Lanham, MD: Rowman & Littlefield.

◆ ◆ ◆ ◆ ◆ ◆

LESSON 12
Radical Politics Made Me Antimotherhood
Ali Michael

Radical politics made me anti- a lot of things. I was antiracist and antioppression, but I was also antimarriage, antidiamonds, anti-heteronormativity, and antimotherhood. I did not want to be some-one's wife. And I did not want to be a pregnant person with all of the social projection that would come with it. I wanted to work for justice. I felt that if I wanted to make the world a better place, having children was not the way to do so.

I felt a shift in that stance on a hot, dusty day in Jericho in the West Bank, when I found myself sitting with a family of 14, sipping tea. I had an internship with the Palestinian Sesame Street, *Shara'a Simsim*, which took me to schools across the West Bank with the Muppet cast of the Sesame Street Workshop franchise. I met teachers, parents, and children for whom the struggle for justice was not "work," not even a "practice," but just a way of life. And even as they lived and worked in struggle, they also had children whom they loved and cherished and whom they taught to live and to love themselves as a form of resistance to all of the anti-Palestinian messaging that exists in the Middle East and the United States. As I sat there with three, maybe four generations, it dawned on me that having children is not a cliché. It is a human experience. It is about surrounding oneself with beloveds for the journey. It is about planting yourself deeply in the earth and committing to care about what happens after you leave. Having children is not the only way to do this and it's not for everyone, but it also does not preclude being radical or making the world a better place.

My daughter was born the following summer.

In my attempt to parent with consciousness, I have held fast to two ideas. The first comes from activist and writer adrienne maree brown (2017), who writes, "The whole is a mirror of the parts. Existence is fractal—the health of the cell is the health of the species and the planet" (p. 13). I take this to mean that my work for justice in the world is just as important as how I organize my life, how I treat people in day-to-day interactions, what I speak about to my children at night. What I do at the personal, individual, cellular level matters just as much as what I say on CNN or write in a book.

The second comes from a blog post I read eight years ago before I had kids that said something along the lines of "White women's liberation has not been at the expense of White men. It has been at the expense of women of color." This is not true across the board, but as my partner and I surveyed our choices for working and raising children, it was clear that the childcare industry was set up to provide me and other middle-class professionals with affordable options at the expense of a low-paid, usually uninsured, almost entirely female, majority people of color childcare workforce. My partner and I both wanted to interrupt this. We did so by committing to a practice called equally shared parenting (Vachon & Vachon, 2010).

Since our children were born, my partner has worked three days/ nights a week, I have worked three days/nights a week, and we split the seventh. Because he is a college rabbi and I teach classes and lead workshops, we have been able to split a workweek that includes weekends and most evenings, leaving each of us about 40 hours a week. I think it is important not to judge these decisions too harshly; parenting is replete with judgment even though—and maybe because—there are not usually a lot of good options. It felt clear to me that there was no obvious antiracist, antisexist choice in how to raise children or where to send them to school. If there was, we would choose it. Most of us are choosing between flawed options in a problematic system. Nevertheless, I see daily examples of individuals finding ways to navigate these flawed options with integrity and humanity. That is what we strove to do. We chose equally shared parenting because it was right for us. That meant spending a lot of time with my kids before they started school.

I worried that committing to spend so much time with children would distract from my work, but as I look back on the past eight years, I realize that it greatly enhanced it. I found that just as I would begin to crash from overload with my work, I could return to a world of play and physical ardor mostly devoid of intellectualism or deep thought. Yet while we played, the questions and dilemmas of my research seemed to work themselves out in my mind, and I would be fresh and motivated when I returned to my desk.

I found myself out in the world in ways I had not been before children—at playgrounds, museums, and schools, where I would observe racial dynamics between others, or between myself and the world, and I would realize how rife the world is with racialized moments that I had not previously noticed because I spent so much time at school and at work. It added incredible layers of richness to my thought process and—I hope—to the final products of my work.

Having children also made me ask the question that has been one of the most compelling of all of my research: What do White children need to know about race? I started the interviews for this project while I was pregnant the first time and continue to write about it eight years later. It has created space for me to ask this question that is central to my parenting and to my deepest values. As my children and their friends grow, I know so much better what the reference points are for parents, what children are developmentally capable of understanding, and I feel comfortable supporting parents of White children who are asking this same question, even as I still seek the answers alongside them.

I never consciously made the choice to become a diversity practitioner. I taught a few classes at my university, I led some workshops, and mostly I wrote. As I finished graduate school, my adviser, Howard Stevenson, recommended me as a consultant to some local schools. After I graduated, I looked for academic jobs, but I had a deep longing to continue to work with teachers in classrooms asking race questions on a daily basis. I found that consulting granted me more freedom to do the research and writing that most interests me while creating materials and workshops that speak to educators and parents. It also allowed the flexibility to be a primary parent to my children (alongside my partner), which involves not only work and joy and exasperation but also the opportunity to teach them what I want them to know about the world. In this way, I hope that I contribute to the health of the species, by way of the cell (half the week)—and to the health of the cell, by way of the species (the other half).

References

brown, a. m. (2017). *Emergent strategy: Shaping change, changing worlds.* Edinburgh, UK: A.K. Press.

Vachon, M., & Vachon, A. (2010). *Equally shared parenting: Rewriting the rules for a new generation of parents.* New York, NY: Perigee.

◆ ◆ ◆ ◆ ◆ ◆

LESSON 13
Global Consulting: Challenges, Opportunities, and Possibilities
Ritu Bhasin

Working as a global diversity consultant opens up a whole new realm for both participants and consultants. The opportunities for growth and change are endless, because there are many areas and issues to explore. Although every nation and community will have diversity strengths, not everyone around the world is working to address their diversity challenges. This gives rise to global diversity consulting work that is complex, nuanced, and meaningful, not to mention a great way to see the world and learn about yourself along the way. The key objectives for anyone who wants to do global work are to gain global diversity experience and knowledge and to focus on positioning yourself as someone who has this expertise.

First, you need an in-depth understanding of diversity and inclusion principles, dynamics, challenges, and issues from around the world, as well as the ability to translate them across different cultures. For example, it is important to be aware not only of the key principles of unconscious bias but also how bias shows up within particular cultures and how it manifests differently across countries. For example, if you are from the United States and want to deliver programming in Nigeria, you will need to learn about Nigerian population demographics, languages, frameworks, cultural identity groups, history, and more, as all these areas will impact your content and how you deliver it.

A second "must do" for a global diversity consultant is to develop your cultural competence—your ability to notice, understand, learn about, and adjust across behavioral differences tied back to culture and cultural identity. Cultural competence is critical for diversity and inclusion. When we are culturally competent, we value behavioral differences that are culturally rooted rather than push behavioral conformity. Given this, cultural competence is essential for teaching diversity and inclusion.

For example, prior to doing extensive diversity and inclusion work in Asia, I worked intently to develop my knowledge and understanding about various Asian cultures. I am of South Asian descent, and I grew up in Canada around many East Asians, which enabled me to apply some of my personal experiences to my teachings. Although leveraging my background was helpful, it was still vastly different compared to working or teaching in Asia.

Before going to Hong Kong for the first time to deliver diversity and inclusion programming, I spent significant time learning from my clients about the various cultural nuances, behaviors, experiences, and issues that are particular to Hong Kong. I also researched Hong Kong workplace culture, combing through diversity-focused research papers, reports, and books to understand these complexities. Through this research and listening to my clients, combined with my ability to understand different behavioral preferences, I became especially knowledgeable about Hong Kong workplace culture, which in turn allowed me to do business within that community.

My last piece of advice is to share the global diversity and inclusion knowledge and tools you have gained through your efforts. Not only does this help communicate your expertise but it also enables you to inspire others to be more knowledgeable about inclusion on a global level.

This is where the real magic happens with this work. If you can expand your cultural competence and share it with others, you will not only engage in personal and professional transformation but also be better positioned to serve your clients and attract future global work, so everyone benefits.

5

Don't Try to Be Big . . . Just Do Big Things!

Eddie Moore Jr., Art Munin, and Marguerite Penick-Parks

W e hope this book has provided both the tangible and reflective components necessary for a successful diversity consultant. The resources are there to help get you started on the journey. Remembering that this is a journey is crucial. We have drawn upon a wealth of experience for this book, yet we are all still making mistakes and developing as we go. There is not a single person in this book (or out of it) who has transcended such difficulties. No matter our years of experience, we are all works in progress.

With that in mind, don't try to be big—just do big things. Being a diversity consultant is about justice, empowerment, inclusion, and equity. It is not just about us. We are merely a tool that, hopefully, provides some insight and guidance along the way. We need colleagues focused on the work and not self-promotion.

In closing, we would like both to summarize some of the major ideas you have read so far and to add a few new ingredients to think about as you move forward. Again, remember, there is no one way to do this work. There is always a need for our further development, so the more you have in your personal cookbook to pull out at a moment's notice, the more we all benefit. Please look at the following points for motivation, thought, reinforcement, challenge, and insight. We hope they guide your launch into the field of diversity consulting in a successful and sustainable way.

Final Takeaways

- Do not let your fear of starting out hold you back. Just go for it!
- Use multiple methods of teaching and engagement in your approach. Additionally, draw important connections between and among justice topics (e.g., race, gender identity, socio-economic status, sexual orientation, immigration status).
- Make power, privilege, and leadership a focal point of your approach.
- Network determines your net worth; never leave home without your promotional materials.
- Work hard, stay focused. There are no shortcuts.
- You should not have to sacrifice core parts of who you are or what you believe. And we all must remember that the person we "burn" today may be the vital contact we need tomorrow.
- Document and copyright everything.
- Remember your strategic plan and your goals, and always return to how to make them sustainable.
- Collaborate with others.
- Making mistakes is an opportunity for growth.
- Within all of the ideas mentioned in *The Diversity Consultant Cookbook,* it is still important to remember you must always push yourself to engage and grow in the work, both in the content of your presentations and in the number of gigs. However, always stay humble and remember those who helped you along the way. We need to remain grateful to each other and support each other while remembering that for many of us this is our livelihood.

Finally, as social justice leaders, we are in this to improve society much more than we are in this to improve us. Every person reading this book is here because he or she wants to make a positive difference. Everyone who wrote for this book did so because he or she, too, wants to make a difference. However, we have to work together. When you are in a good place, pay it forward and help someone else. Be Kind. Be Collaborative. Be Honest. Be True.

Conclusion—Lesson 14:
Fourteen Staple Ingredients in My Consulting Kitchen

Peggy McIntosh

In doing hundreds of presentations and consultations over the last 35 years, I have found that keeping the following 14 ingredients in stock serves me well.

Ingredient 1: Preparing

When I am invited to an institution, I make a point of talking ahead of time to find out from people there what led to my invitation as a speaker or consultant. If I ask empathetic questions, I can learn a lot about the health and vital signs of the institution and the triggering symptoms or events that led to the invitation. I may discover some people's quite specific needs and hopes. Often those who drive me from an airport to a speaking site can tell me a lot about why I have been invited. I aim to strengthen the hand of those who are suffering most and to leave everyone feeling equally human.

Ingredient 2: Finding Alternatives to Slideshows

In presenting my interactive phase theory, I found drawing it out on a whiteboard more effective than a slideshow. So now, I find ways to illustrate physically the metaphors of most of my talks. I create Möbius strips to illustrate the Feeling Like a Fraud papers. I talk as I spell out the process of my thinking. Often I distribute brief handouts that get to the heart of my presentation. These are written in a way that allows the audience to use the concepts from my presentation in their own lives or work. I direct the audience to the National SEED Project website, where they can find the White Privilege papers. My diagrammatic presentations often give the audience members something accessible and tangible to carry away.

Ingredient 3: Making Introductions More Engaging

Hearing speakers' credentials read aloud often sends me to sleep, so I ask those who will introduce me to tell the audience the meaning of the event to them, personally. After all, the audience knows that person and cannot know me through my curriculum vitae. My talk itself will need to earn whatever respect I may get.

Ingredient 4: Interacting

Dividing a group into smaller groups allows the participants to get to know each others' experiences. I avoid lecturing but set prompts that frame the interactions. Setting careful prompts requires more thought than anything else in a session and often requires quick revisioning and intuitive realigning based on the dynamics of the group. I time interactions quite tightly, often using one or two minutes as the limit. For me, interacting also takes the form of going out into the audience during a session to get more face time with individuals who wish to comment or question. Another form of interacting comes afterward, when I stay to see everyone who wishes to talk further (or take a selfie), even if this delays attending a reception or an event.

Ingredient 5: Doing Serial Testimony

In serial testimony, each person in a group speaks about his or her own experience of the topic at hand—not *opinions*, but *actual experiences*. The group size can be as small as two or as large as might seem reasonable. Victor Lewis and I developed this method when consulting at the College of New Jersey in 2000. The process asks people to speak in a given order, in response to a specific prompt, and with time limits. As a result, speakers become amazingly focused and to the point. A strong prompt is one that has a clear orientation and, at the same time, allows for an expanded, not expansive, response. In serial testimony, everyone in the room will be heard, and everyone will speak, unless they choose not to. There is no interrupting, no arguing, and no direct reference to what anyone else has said. When a few people say the same thing, this usually illuminates a pattern in society. There is no chance to take sides and form cabals. A consultant to Seeking Educational Equity and Diversity (SEED), Reverend Linda Powell Pruitt, once reminded us on the subject of anything at all that we were discussing: "The data is in the room" (see nationalseedproject.org for more on this project). What I find is that when the data are in the room , listeners can become their own theorists from the examples that they are hearing and offering. I tell audience members that each of them is a walking encyclopedia of personal experience, and they're still building it every day.

Ingredient 6: Having the Audience Create the Agenda

In the 1980s, I was asked to give a 2-hour faculty development session for faculty at Pasadena Polytechnic High School in California. I felt I needed to know more about the region, the people, and the institution. I told the audience of faculty and staff that I wanted them to make 19 comments (I chose this figure arbitrarily) on anything that was on their minds about making curriculum and teaching methods more inclusive. I did not respond on the spot to any of the 19 comments but made quick notes on each. It took an hour to gather these comments. Then we had a 10-minute break with refreshments, during which I pulled together some threads. I spent the final 50 minutes of the session making some kind of response to each of the comments. I noted what each commentator was wearing and where they were sitting, so I could respond to them 1-on-1. Since that first use of the "19-question format," I and other members of the SEED Project have developed it further, especially for conference settings. The first question is restated and then responded to by an individual or members of a panel; this pattern continues until all 19 questions are addressed.

Ingredient 7: Practicing Mental Journeying Rather Than Aiming for Fixed Knowledge

I have been strongly influenced by something said by Virginia Woolf (1931). When she was asked to Oxford and Cambridge Universities to speak about "Women and Fiction," she said of this topic,

> One cannot hope to tell the truth. One can only show how one came to hold whatever opinion one does hold. One can only give one's audience the chance of drawing their own conclusions as they observe the limitations, the prejudices, the idiosyncrasies of the speaker. (p.1)

In my consulting and speaking, I tell people how I came to *my* thoughts about something—feelings of fraudulence, or having privilege, or noticing types of curriculum and pedagogy that may create or discourage in the student feelings of belonging and mattering. I think watching a mind recount its mental and emotional journeys is what keeps audiences alert and present during my sessions. Some people can track their own mental and emotional journeys more easily after hearing me speak. By the same token, when consulting, instead of giving advice, I talk about how I deal with situations and dilemmas that are relevant to what is being discussed. This can be seen as overly narrow, but at least it is not overreaching. Staying personal and vulnerable gives me credibility and can also relax the egos of those who have been feeling accused, encouraging them to feel less defensive and more open.

Ingredient 8: Copresenting

Many times, instead of discussing diversity, equity, or inclusion by myself, I ask to copresent with people of color, to share the time, the money, or the attention from the institution's publicity department. Negotiating the internal public relations and external press coverage of the event is the hardest part of this exercise. I work closely with public relations personnel to try to give equal time, space, and attention to White people and to people of color, whether they are local or from outside the institution. Sometimes the hardest work of the preparation is ensuring that the written program honors all of the speakers equally. It is so easy for White privilege to prevail in the publicity.

Ingredient 9: Not Taking the Audiovisual Staff for Granted

I appreciate the audiovisual staff. The quality of my talk will be strongly affected by how well they deploy their equipment. Auditoriums and mics have quirks, and the audiovisual staff know this better than anyone. I am especially pleased if my talk or panel captures the attention of the audiovisual staff, for they have heard many talks in their time.

Ingredient 10: Realizing There Is No Need to Please Everyone

I used to notice if a person was sitting at the back of an auditorium, ostentatiously and elaborately opening and reading his or her snail mail as if to say, "They made me come to this, but I am not really here." I used to work on turning that person around to the point that he or she put down the papers and began to listen. I could usually do it, and I felt good about that, but I now think it was not worth the trouble. I am less concerned now about appealing to everyone and more determined to include everyone. If I can manage the interactive elements well, no one must feel in the position of being an individual resistor.

Ingredient 11: Recognizing Changes in Institutions

If I have been to an institution previously and received an invitation to return, I make a point of appreciating the changes that have taken place since I last visited. It helps to locate the institution in history, to hear itself talked about as worth following in the developments it is engineering for itself. Whether or not I am on a return visit, it is useful to have read some of the recent publications coming out of the university or school. Many institutions have been working for decades on inclusiveness. It is insulting when a consultant uses the phrase "We must begin" to work on this or that, as if the institution or members of the institution have not already begun.

Ingredient 12: Trusting the Inner Life of Students

When I speak about my faith that students can understand their own deep experience, which is unique to them and on which they are the only experts in the world, the audience becomes quiet. Fidgeting stops. I see this as a spiritual shift toward taking themselves seriously. Perhaps it is the best gift I can bring and the most lasting. Now that people of the right and alt-right are taking themselves more seriously than they have in the last several decades, I am afraid. Perhaps I have had too much faith in the inner life of most people. But I think when they are helped to understand *social structures around them and in them at the same time*, they are intellectually nourished and can resist the extreme individualism, egotism, arrogance, deception, and violence that are emanating from the far right and being licensed by it.

Ingredient 13: Citing Others

I make sure to cite the work of everybody whom I reference and others who have strongly influenced my work and thought during my talks or consultancies. I don't like to deluge people with titles, authors, and films they haven't seen, but I want to imply that in fields such as privilege, which I discuss, there is a great deal of activity going on, and each of us in the field owes many intellectual debts to others.

Ingredient 14: Sending Appreciation

Often sponsors take quite a risk when they invite me. I thank them for their commitment, courage, and work securing the funds for the event.

In closing, Eddie Moore and his coeditors have asked us to sum up some of our experiences, our successes, and our new learnings. My general experience is that travel to schools is a lot of fun. Most students who attend my talks are serious and committed to social change. They are thirsting for conversation; they deserve to be taken seriously by themselves and by adults as the way of the future, which they are. The staff and faculty who invite me have moral staying power, even in these bad times. I admire their courage and persistence.

What are my successes? I will never know. I am most gratified by being thanked for my work. An older faculty member may say, "I first heard you in 1986. Our department was never the same." Sometimes a success is being able to become friends with people who attend my talk. Occasionally, faculty band together to get the university to give me an honorary degree. This draws public attention to the fact that a university is taking on brave work on systemic change. It widens the horizon for such antiracism work and strengthens the members of the university who are leading the work toward change.

References

McIntosh, P. (1985). *Feeling like a fraud.* Wellesley, MA: Wellesley Centers for Women.

McIntosh, P. (1988). *White privilege and male privilege: A personal account of coming to see correspondences through work in women's studies.* Wellesley, MA: Wellesley Centers for Women.

Woolf, V. (1931). *A room of one's own.* London, UK: Hogarth Press.

Afterword

Working with diversity consultants for nearly 30 years has given me invaluable life lessons that I use every day, both personally and professionally. Diversity consultants radiate an inner passion for educating others with a common vision of transforming this world into a better place— truly an admirable calling.

Unfortunately for many consultants, their hard work and dedication often do not produce the results or impact that they desire. Some focus more on their mission than on their business, which hinders growth and progress.

If you really want to maximize the impact you have on the world, start with a Growth Recipe™. This 3-step process leverages 10 of the most effective "ingredients" that have been proven to grow and scale hundreds of other businesses.

Step One: Identify

A solid strategy is the key to success and aligning your efforts and resources. Knowledge is power, so to craft your Growth Recipe™, start by gathering these valuable insights, your ingredients for success.

Ingredient #1: Key Stakeholders

Identify who the most important stakeholders are for your business (clients, prospects, referral sources, etc.). What is of highest priority to *them* (cost, timing, logistics, politics, etc.), and how can you best engage these individuals (events, social media, phone, e-mail, etc.)?

Ingredient #2: Tiers of Competition

Don't just rely on Google for competitive intelligence. Instead, seek names from colleagues on prospects who are looking for consultants, and ask about speakers they see as your competition. And don't stop there—dig deeper to uncover the hidden second tier of your competition that is often a larger barrier to success. This tier may include factors such as budget concerns, procrastination, unwillingness to engage with new ideas, internal politics, and other similar obstacles you must overcome.

Ingredient #3 and Ingredient #4: SMART Goals and SWOT

If you are unfamiliar with SMART and SWOT, Google them, because they are critical. Be sure to organize your goals into specific categories, and include business, financial, personal, spiritual, health, and anything else that is meaningful to you. Very importantly, don't SWOT alone! Since it's almost impossible to be objective about oneself, ask others for their external views. Ask them to be critically honest, this is the time you want their tough love.

Step Two: Create

Once you've reviewed the competitive intelligence and market insights and updated your goals accordingly, you can begin to develop tools to support your outreach and marketing efforts.

Ingredient #5: Brand Messaging

In today's overcluttered world, it's critical that your message breaks through to your audience. To do this, position your services as a BUM:

- *B*elievable to the world: Be able to support your claims.
- *U*niquely differentiated: Separate yourself from the competition.
- *M*otivating to your key audience: Get them to act now.

Ingredient #6: Stay Open

While you can't ignore the benefits and power of digital and social media, do not underestimate the potential results you may see from traditional and experiential marketing (again, look up *experiential marketing* if the term is unfamiliar). Evaluate any solution that matches your strategy and supports your goals. That may mean taking a break from Facebook to attend a live event or even send a personal handwritten letter. You may be amazed at the results.

Ingredient #7: Heart and Mind

Good business communication focuses on tangible benefits, and great communications also speak to clients' emotions. As humans, we try our best to make logical decisions through analysis, but studies show that nearly 90% of all decisions are made or influenced by emotions. Take the time to know what's in the heart of your audience, and you'll find that their minds will follow.

Step Three: Grow

Now that you have the strategy and tools to succeed, you're ready to start growing your business. Here comes the fun part!

Ingredient #8: Two Are Better Than One

Being a solo practitioner can be a lonely road, but collaborating with others can greatly increase your opportunities. Find noncompetitive companies or individuals that are serving the same audience as your business, and meet with them to discuss and explore synergies.

Ingredient #9: Always Be Tracking

If you can't measure it, you can't grow it. List out your key performance indicators, such as how many prospects you have reached, the conversion rate, whether evaluations lead to repeat business, and so on. Once you quantify what actions are needed to achieve your goals, break them down to monthly or weekly milestones so you can monitor, measure and make regular adjustments.

Ingredient #10: Love the Numbers

Few diversity consultants started off as accountants, but it's absolutely mandatory that you know your numbers better than anyone. How many meetings does it take to sign up a client? What's the average annual revenue and lifetime value per customer? What are your gross and net margins? What's your close ratio? Trying to grow a business without this information is like asking a pilot to fly a plane without any gauges. It's certainly possible, but it seems like a recipe for disaster.

Finally, when following this Growth Recipe™ feel free to experiment and add any other "ingredients" to make it your own!

Here's to great growing!

Joey Iazzetto
Chief Growth Officer
ICG Marketing
www.icgmarketing.com

About the Editors and Contributors

Editors

Eddie Moore Jr., PhD, founded America & Moore LLC (eddie moorejr.com) in 1996. Moore is recognized as one of the nation's top motivational speakers/educators, especially for his work with K–16 students. Recent challenges in the country have found Moore being in demand for work with law enforcement, higher education, city employees, and businesses searching to improve the inclusive environments of their workplaces. Moore is also the founder and program director for the White Privilege Conference (WPC). Under the direction of Moore and his inclusive relationship model, the WPC has become one of the top national and international conferences for participants who want to move beyond dialogue and into action around issues of diversity, power, privilege, and leadership. In 2014 Moore founded the Privilege Institute, a not-for-profit organization that engages people in research, education, action, and leadership through workshops, conferences, publications, and strategic partnerships and relationships. Moore is cofounder of the online journal *Understanding and Dismantling Privilege* and coeditor of *Everyday White People Confront Racial and Social Injustice: 15 Stories* (Stylus, 2015) as well as *The Guide for White Women Who Teach Black Boys* (Corwin Press, 2017).

Art Munin, PhD, has served as a diversity educator and consultant for institutions across the United States for 15 years through his company Art Munin Consulting (artmunin.com). He currently serves as associate vice chancellor and dean of students at the University of Wisconsin Oshkosh. Munin has coathored chapters in the books *Closing the Opportunity Gap: Identity-Conscious Strategies for Retention and Student Success* (Stylus, 2016) and *Handbook for Student Leadership Development* (Jossey-Bass, 2011). His first book is *Color by Number: Understanding Racism Through Facts and Stats on Children* (Stylus, 2012). As a complement to this work, Munin has served in

---

Publisher's Note

Editors have been listed alphabetically.

several capacities through NASPA, including the chair of the Assistant/ Associate Vice President (AVP) Steering Committee, AVP Institute faculty, associate editor for *Journal of Student Affairs Research and Practice*, a member of the Civic Learning and Democratic Engagement Initiative, and a member of the regional conference planning committee.

Marguerite Penick-Parks, PhD, prepares preservice teachers in the areas of multicultural education, culturally responsive pedagogy, and social justice. Her work centers on issues of power, privilege, and oppression in relationship to issues of curriculum, with a special emphasis on the incorporation of quality literature. She appears in the movie *Mirrors of Privilege: Making Whiteness Visible* (World Trust Organization, 2006). Her most recent work is a joint article on creating safe spaces for discussing White privilege with preservice teachers, and she is a coeditor of *Everyday White People Confronting Racial and Social Injustice: 15 Stories* (Stylus, 2015) and *The Guide for White Women Who Teach Black Boys* (Corwin Press, 2017).

Contributors

Devon Alexander has lived in the northwest suburban area of Chicago, Illinois. Given his lived experience of race within American society and the American educational system, it's fitting that Alexander grew up in the suburban Chicagoland area immortalized in John Hughes's films like *Ferris Bueller's Day Off, The Breakfast Club,* and *Sixteen Candles.* Alexander grew up as a young male of color immersed in an environment that did not reflect his lived experiences of race. It was in schools that he became increasingly conscious of the disparity between his developing racial consciousness and the people with whom he inhabited these predominantly White spaces. As a racial equity coach, he works with the hope of infiltrating the American educational system as someone who interrupts the systemic racial educational disparities that ravage the lives within these systems, especially people of color. Alexander works to reveal the intersections of race, racism, Whiteness, and education.

Jacqueline Battalora, PhD, is a keynote speaker, an author, trainer, and a consultant in workplace and educational inclusion. Her keynotes about the legal invention of the human category "White people" turn contemporary conceptions of race upside down and reorient thinking about race and human divisions. The keynotes are steeped in law and history made both accessible and nuanced. They are engaging, thought-provoking, and relevant. The keynotes provide attendees with immediate actions and longer term processes for transforming their lives, workplaces, and communities into a strong reflection of belonging and equal opportunity. Battalora is the author of *Birth of a White Nation: The Invention of White People and Its Relevance Today* (Strategic Book Publishing & Rights Agency, 2013). She is an attorney and a professor of sociology at Saint Xavier University, Chicago, and a former Chicago police officer. Battalora is also an editor for *Journal of Understanding and Dismantling Privilege.*

Ritu Bhasin, LLB, MBA, president of bhasin consulting inc. (bhasinconsulting.com), is an award-winning speaker, author, and globally recognized expert in diversity and inclusion, women's advancement, and authentic leadership. Since 2010, Bhasin has delivered leadership training, coaching, and advisory services across sectors, working with top organizations and senior leadership teams around the world to develop inclusive cultures. Bhasin is known for her expertise in cultural competence, unconscious bias, and neuroscience strategies and has coached hundreds of leaders and executives to be more inclusive. Bhasin's Amazon best-selling book, *The Authenticity Principle* (Melanin Made Press, 2017), was released in the fall of 2017. In the same year, Bhasin also coauthored a groundbreaking research study called Sponsor Effect: Canada, with the Center for Talent Innovation, which examines the experiences that people of color, Indigenous peoples, and women have with advocacy and sponsorship in the workplace. To learn more about Bhasin, visit ritubhasin.com. Follow Bhasin on Facebook at authenticityprinciple and on Twitter and Instagram @ritu_bhasin.

Diane J. Goodman, EdD, has been addressing diversity and social justice issues as an educator and activist for more than 30 years. She speaks, trains, and consults nationally and internationally with a wide range of organizations, community groups, schools, and universities. Goodman has been a professor at several universities in the areas of education, psychology, social work, and women's studies. She is the author of the book *Promoting Diversity and Social Justice: Educating People From Privileged Groups* (second edition, Routledge, 2011) and coeditor and cocontributor to *Teaching for Diversity and Social Justice* (third edition, Routledge,

2016) as well as other publications. For more about her, see her website (www.dianegoodman.com).

Joey Iazzetto has pioneered and grown more than 100 successful start-ups and established businesses over his 30-year career. His work with global enterprise organizations including Verizon, GE, Motorola, and Mercedes Benz has received national recognition and earned multiple industry awards. After cofounding UniCom Marketing Group in 1995, Iazzeto served as national chairman of MENG and lead the integration to create the American Marketing Association Executive Circle. He is a featured speaker at Northwestern University/Kellogg School of Management, University of Chicago/Booth School of Business, and numerous television and radio programs. Iazzetto is currently the chief growth officer of ICG Marketing, helping companies identify profitable opportunities, create measurable solutions, and grow revenue and profitability.

John Igwebuike (Ig-wih-bee-kay), PhD, JD, academic, autodidact, attorney, author, and advocate, is interim provost and executive vice president for academic affairs at Alcorn State University. He has held positions as vice provost, registrar, dean of graduate studies, dean of business, and National Collegiate Athletic Association faculty athletics representative. He is a tenured professor of legal environment of business. He has served as management team leader for Kimberly-Clark Corporation, assistant director at the Ohio Commission on African-American Males, and trainer for Mentorship Columbus. He is founder of Guanacaste: The Lead Listening Institute. Guanacaste is a quiet revolution—a unique movement—dedicated to advancing and championing the positive power of effective listening communication to transform individuals, relationships, organizations, and society. Guanacaste trains, equips, and develops lead listening champions in schools, corporations, nonprofit organizations, churches, communities, and universities. He earned his PhD from Ohio State University and JD from Indiana University–Indianapolis.

Peggy McIntosh works at the Wellesley Centers for Women at Wellesley College. In 1987, she founded, and for 25 years codirected with Emily Style, the National SEED Project on Inclusive Curriculum (Seeking Educational Equity and Diversity). She consults widely in the

United States and throughout the world on creating inclusive curricula and classrooms. In 1988, she published the groundbreaking article "White Privilege and Male Privilege: A Personal Account of Coming to See Correspondences Through Work on Women's Studies." This analysis and its shorter form, "White Privilege: Unpacking the Invisible Knapsack" (1989), have been instrumental in putting the dimension of privilege into discussions of power, gender, race, and sexuality in the United States. Her other articles on privilege include "White Privilege, Color and Crime" (1998), "White Privilege: An Account to Spend" (2009), and "White People Facing Race: Five Myths That Keep Racism in Place" (2009). Routledge will publish a collection of her essays in 2019.

Ali Michael, PhD, is the cofounder and director of the Race Institute for K–12 Educators and the author of *Raising Race Questions: Whiteness and Inquiry in Education* (Teachers College Press, 2015), winner of the 2017 Society of Professors of Education Outstanding Book Award. She is coeditor of the bestselling *Everyday White People Confront Racial and Social Injustice: 15 Stories* (Stylus, 2015) and bestselling *Guide for White Women Who Teach Black Boys* (Corwin Press, 2017). She also sits on the editorial board of the journal *Whiteness and Education*. Michael's article "What Do White Children Need to Know About Race?", coauthored with Eleonora Bartoli in *Independent Schools Magazine*, won the Association and Media Publishing Gold Award for Best Feature Article in 2014. She may be best known for her November 9, 2016, piece "What Do We Tell the Children?" in the *Huffington Post*. For more details, see alimichael.org.

Sumun L. Pendakur, EdD, is the chief learning officer and director of the University of Southern California (USC) Equity Institutes at the USC Race and Equity Center, dedicated to advancing racial justice in higher education and other sectors. Prior to this position, Pendakur was the assistant vice president for diversity and inclusion at Harvey Mudd College and as the director for USC Asian Pacific American Student Services. Pendakur is a consultant, speaker, and facilitator, helping campuses, nonprofits, and other organizations build capacity for cultural competence, social justice, and equitable practices. She is a scholar-practitioner whose research interests and publications focus on critical race theory, Asian American and Pacific Islander students, change agents, and institutional transformation. Pendakur is a graduate of Northwestern University with a double major in women's studies and history and a minor in Spanish. She holds a master's in higher education administration from the University of Michigan. She received her doctorate in higher education leadership from the USC Rossier School of Education.

Vijay Pendakur, PhD, serves as the Robert W. and Elizabeth C. Staley Dean of Students at Cornell University. Prior to this appointment, he worked on campus-wide student success initiatives for underserved populations as an associate vice president for student affairs at California State University–Fullerton. Before joining the team at Fullerton, Pendakur served as the director for the Office of Multicultural Student Success at DePaul University in Chicago. He is the editor of the recent book *Closing the Opportunity Gap: Identity-Conscious Strategies for Retention and Student Success* (Stylus, 2016), as well as numerous chapters on Asian American racial identity development, color-blind racism, and critical leadership pedagogy. He holds a bachelor's degree in history and East Asian studies from the University of Wisconsin–Madison, a master's degree in U.S. history from the University of California–San Diego, and a doctorate of education from DePaul University.

Dena Samuels, PhD, an award-winning faculty member at the University of Colorado, now serves full-time as a mindfulness-based diversity, equity, and inclusion leadership development consultant, public speaker, and inspiration coach around the United States. Her latest book, *The Mindfulness Effect: An Unexpected Journey to Healing, Connection, & Social Justice* (Night River Press, 2018), offers 25 mindfulness practices for healing, self-empowerment, culturally inclusive leadership, and social and environmental justice. Her previous book, *The Culturally Inclusive Educator: Preparing for a Multicultural World* (Teachers College Press, 2014), provides transformative inquiry and strategies for building cultural inclusiveness. Through her keynotes and workshops on implicit bias and microaggressions, she assists organizations, campuses, and corporations in building more diverse, equitable, and inclusive cultures. Samuels volunteers as cofacilitator of the Second Tuesday Race Forum of Denver and serves on the board of the Privilege Institute, the institutional home of the annual White Privilege Conference.

Bryant K. Smith is a man with a vision. He is an expert in identifying, cultivating, and maximizing human potential. For more than two decades Smith's work has been at the forefront of assisting business, athletic, and educational institutions in recruiting, training, and retaining top talent. His inspirational keynotes, engaging seminars, and insightful coaching deliver measurable results, improve communication and performance, and change lives for the better. Smith is the author of nine books, including a social commentary on race relations in the United States entitled *Black Not Blind* (Voice of Truths, 2002), a book about the power of human potential entitled *Five* (CreateSpace Independent Publishing Platform, 2012), and four books on male development. Founder of the Remix Hip Hop Leadership Institute and president and CEO of SmithCAN, a comprehensive consulting and training company, Smith is a highly sought after lecturer known for his ability to get his audience to critically think about complex issues, find their purpose, and make a difference in the world. For more information about Smith and his work, go to smithcan.com.

Orinthia Swindell has had a lifelong passion for learning and teaching others about equity and inclusion work. She has served as an early childhood educator for more than 20 years and is currently the director of equity and inclusion at an independent school in her hometown, Brooklyn, New York, in addition to her role as an independent consultant. Swindell has facilitated numerous workshops and presentations, presented at national conferences, and been a guest speaker at teacher preparation programs. One of her most esteemed accomplishments is being the mother of two amazing Black young men. See orinthiaswindell.com for more information.

Vernon A. Wall has accumulated more than 30 years of professional student affairs experience at Iowa State University; the University of Georgia; the University of North Carolina (UNC)–Charlotte; and UNC–Chapel Hill, with experience in Greek life, new student orientation, student activities, leadership development, global education, and university housing. Vernon currently lives in Washington DC and is the director for business development at LeaderShape, Inc. Wall is also president and founder of One Better World, LLC—a consulting firm specializing in engaging others in courageous social justice and equity conversations. With degrees from North Carolina State University and

Indiana University, Wall is the consummate scholar-practitioner. He has received several awards for his contributions to the quality of student life, is a nationally known speaker in the areas of social justice and leadership, and is one of the founders and facilitators of the Social Justice Training Institute. See vernonwall.org, sjti.org, and leadershape .org for more information.

Jamie Washington, PhD, MDiv, is the president and founder of the Washington Consulting Group. Washington has served as an educator, administrator, and consultant in higher education for more than 34 years. He is the president and cofounder of the Social Justice Training Institute and the president of the American College Personnel Association. He also serves as the pastor of Unity Fellowship Church of Baltimore and is an elder in the Unity Fellowship Church Movement.

Tim Wise is among the nation's most prominent antiracist essayists and educators and the author of seven books, including his highly acclaimed memoir, *White Like Me: Reflections on Race From a Privileged Son* (Soft Skull Press, 2011), as well as *Dear White America: Letter to a New Minority* (City Lights Publishers, 2012) and *Under the Affluence: Shaming the Poor, Praising the Rich and Sacrificing the Future of America* (City Lights Publishers, 2015). Wise is featured in, and cowrote, two documentary films: *The Great White Hoax: Donald Trump and the Politics of Race and Class in America* (2017) and *White Like Me: Race, Racism and White Privilege in America* (2013), both from the Media Education Foundation. Additionally, he hosts the biweekly podcast *Speak Out With Tim Wise*, featuring interviews with activists, scholars, and artists about movement building and strategies for social change.

The Authors

This cookbook is built on a knowledge base of 60 years of combined work in the areas of diversity and social justice research, consultation, and teaching in K–12 and postsecondary education, community, and the corporate arena by the principal authors. Each brings a different strength to the work, and like all issues of diversity consulting, it is the multiple perspectives that bring strength to the final product.

INDEX

"Simply put, socialized biased behaviors are difficult to transform; however, being armed with stories and data may help persuade some that things need to change if we are going to save the next generation of children of color. I hope that everyone is willing to be a change agent after reading this book." — ***Mary Howard-Hamilton***, *Holmstedt Distinguished Professor, Higher Education Program, Indiana State University*

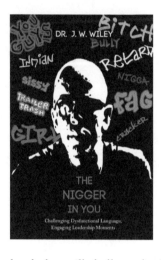

The Nigger in You

Challenging Dysfunctional Language, Engaging Leadership Moments

J.W. Wiley

"Employing arguably the most polarizing epithet in American history, nigger, Dr. J. W. Wiley grabs the attention of those who understand the castigation of racism, but who may not grasp the multiple ways that otherness beyond race is treated in contemporary American culture. *The Nigger in You* is a spellbinding book that will challenge both the newcomer to diversity studies as well as the veteran of social justice." — ***Thomas Keith,*** *Professor, California State Polytechnic University–Pomona, and Filmmaker ("Generation M: Misogyny in Media & Culture" and "The Bro Code")*

"This book is inspiring, challenging, informative, and a timeless resource for educators, parents, and community leaders. It's the real deal. You'll learn something every time you read it." — ***Eddie Moore Jr.,*** *Founder/Director, The White Privilege Conference*

22883 Quicksilver Drive

Sterling, VA 20166-2019   Subscribe to our e-mail alerts: www.Styluspub.com

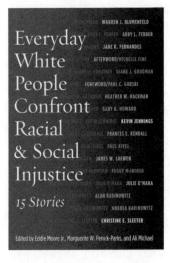

(Continues on preceding page)